ETHICS AT WORK

BASIC READINGS IN BUSINESS ETHICS

WILLIAM H. SHAW

Department of Philosophy
San Jose State University

New York   Oxford
OXFORD UNIVERSITY PRESS
2003

Oxford University Press

Oxford   New York
Auckland   Bangkok   Buenos Aires   Cape Town
Chennai   Dar es Salaam   Delhi   Hong Kong   Istanbul   Karachi
Kolkata   Kuala Lumpur   Madrid   Melbourne   Mexico City   Mumbai
Nairobi   São Paulo   Shanghai   Taipei   Tokyo   Toronto

Copyright © 2003 by Oxford University Press, Inc.

Published by Oxford University Press, Inc.
198 Madison Avenue, New York, New York, 10016
http://www.oup-usa.org

Oxford is a registered trademark of Oxford University Press

Library of Congress Cataloging-in-Publication Data

Ethics at work : basic readings in business ethics / [edited by] William H. Shaw.
    p. cm.
    Includes bibliographical references.
    ISBN 0-19-513942-9 (pbk.)
    1. Business ethics.   I. Shaw, William H., 1948–

HF5387 .E836 2002
174'.4—dc21

                                                                    2002074883

9   8   7   6   5   4   3   2   1

Printed in the United States of America
on acid-free paper

CONTENTS

PREFACE

Without widespread adherence to certain moral norms, no economic system can function, let alone provide the foundation for a prosperous and just society. Few people would deny this truth or the importance and social relevance of the study of business ethics. These days almost all universities teach the subject, often requiring their students to take it because of its significance to their lives and to the future of our society.

As an academic field, business ethics is an applied subject. Oriented toward real-world problems, it addresses concrete but challenging moral issues in people's business and professional lives and in our business system itself. These issues it tackles in an eclectic spirit, drawing freely on different academic fields and various intellectual resources as questions of business practice and economic policy intertwine with topics in politics, sociology, and organizational theory. At its heart, however, business ethics remains anchored in philosophy. Despite the relevance and undeniable utility of empirical studies of business behavior, at the end of the day the foundational task of business ethics is to wrestle with the difficult ethical or normative questions that business gives rise to. These are exactly the kind of questions that have been, at least since Socrates, the distinctive province of philosophy. Moreover, business ethics approaches these questions with the argumentative, conceptual, and theoretical tools that characterize contemporary philosophical practice.

Ethics at Work is a compact collection of good, solid essays in business ethics written by well respected authors, essays that display the importance of the enterprise and its fundamentally moral and philosophical character. Although the general reader can learn much from it, the book is designed as a textbook for use in university-level courses on business ethics, business and society, contemporary moral issues, and related subjects. To this end, the essays have been chosen, not only because of their intellectual merit, but also because of their pedagogical strengths. All of the essays are well written. Tackling provocative issues that students will find engaging and important, the essays should provide a lively springboard for classroom discussion. Moreover, they have been carefully edited and abridged to make them more accessible to student readers (as opposed to the academic or professional audience for which they were originally written). The essays are prefaced by short introductions with study questions to guide students in their reading, and they are followed by review and discussion questions along with suggestions for further reading. The essays presuppose no prior knowledge of philosophy.

The first two essays provide an introductory overview. Roger Crisp explains the nature and philosophical character of business ethics, defending the subject against various criticisms, and turning students' attention to the fact that philosophy is inescapable once we pause to reflect on the nature and justification of our conduct. J. R. Lucas then outlines the basic moral responsibilities of businesspeople. He shows how these responsibilities (which, he argues, extend beyond the pursuit of profit) grow out of the social role and function of business, and he discusses their specific nature and extent in different areas.

The essays in part two take on specific topics in business ethics, beginning with downsizing and the use of overseas sweatshops, and going on to cover such issues as bribery, whistle blowing, drug testing, deception in sales, manipulative advertising, insider trading, and the environment. The essays represent diverse ethical and philosophical orientations, and no one school of moral thought is favored over any other. All of the authors display the virtues that philosophy seeks to cultivate. Instead of preaching or issuing polemics, they approach their topics in an honest and open-minded way, striving for clarity, accuracy, and intellectual fairness. They reason carefully and rigorously, attending closely to the arguments both for and against their positions. Although each essay is self-contained and although the various essays address different (although often related) topics, rather than following a simple for-and-against format, the reader will find interesting connections and illuminating contrasts between the arguments of the different authors.

There are many ways to teach business ethics, and instructors will inevitably have diverse philosophical perspectives, teaching goals, and instructional techniques. Given its compactness, the range of issues it treats, and the quality of its essays, *Ethics at Work* can fit well with various class plans, course materials, and teaching styles, and it can work well in varied classroom settings and with different kinds of students.

CHAPTER ONE

A Defence of Philosophical Business Ethics

Roger Crisp

Roger Crisp, Fellow and Tutor in Philosophy at St. Anne's College, Oxford, argues that businesspeople are wrong to ignore moral philosophy. After distinguishing different senses of "business ethics," Crisp responds to those who reject business ethics on egoistic or skeptical grounds, and he defends the subject against the charge that it is abstract, irrelevant, and mired in irresolvable disagreements. Philosophy is difficult to escape because when people stop to think about their conduct, they are seeking to justify the course of action they eventually choose—that is, they are doing philosophy. Although it needs to be informed by an understanding of real business problems, business ethics, as a philosophical discipline, has its own independent and important role to play in our society.

THINGS TO CONSIDER

1. What are the three senses of "business ethics" that Crisp distinguishes?
2. What is egoism, and why does Crisp say that it is "hard to believe"?
3. How does Crisp respond to the argument that there is no truth in ethics because different societies have often accepted different moral principles?
4. Some businesspeople believe that philosophy is too abstract to help us deal with real-life problems in business. What two responses does Crisp make to this objection?
5. What does Crisp mean when he writes that much "contemporary moral philosophy, business ethics included, operates on a mistaken scientific model"?

Reprinted by permission from Christopher Cowton and Roger Crisp, eds., *Business Ethics: Perspectives on the Practice of Theory* (Oxford: Oxford University Press, 1998). Notes omitted.

1. BUSINESS ETHICS

What is meant by "business ethics"? The phrase is sometimes used to refer to the ethical outlook, whether implied by behaviour or explicitly stated, of a company or individual engaged in business. Behaviour and statement can of course come apart, so that one might say of a certain corporation: "Their ethic is allegedly one of service to the community, but their woeful environmental record shows what they really believe."

In a second sense, business ethics is that set of principles or reasons which should govern the conduct of business, whether at the individual or collective level. If we assume that there are many ways in which people should not act in business, business ethics in this second sense refers to the way people *should* act.

In its final, and most commonly used, sense, business ethics is an area of philosophical enquiry, with its own topics of discussion, specialists, journals, centres, and of course a panoply of different ethical positions. In this sense, I suggest, business ethics refers to the philosophical endeavours of human beings to grasp the principles constituting business ethics in its second sense, usually with the idea that these should become the "ethic" of real businesses and business people.

Philosophers have long thought about philosophy and its nature. The Platonic Socrates saw philosophy as preparation for death, while Aristotle viewed philosophy as the activity in engaging in which we are most like the gods. I shall not make a claim anywhere near as grand, but will suggest that philosophical business ethics is the best way we know to approach the truth about how our economic and business life should be. I shall proceed largely by fending off objections to philosophical business ethics, but the positive advantages of the practice should emerge as we go.

2. PHILOSOPHICAL SCEPTICISM

Philosophical scepticism is almost as old as philosophical reflection itself, and scepticism about the claims of morality or ethics as old as any form of scepticism. According to the sceptic, philosophical business ethics is misguided, and indeed pointless, because what it seeks is a chimera. There are no principles for philosophical business ethics to uncover.

There are several forms of this kind of scepticism. According to the first, egoism, we do indeed have reasons for action, but they are all egoistic or self-referring reasons. Ethics concerns my relations to others and the environment, but in fact rationality suggests that I should govern such relations only in accordance with my own self-interest. This kind of objection is particularly likely to emerge in business ethics, since business is often taken to be a paradigmatically self-interested enterprise.

According to one moral theory common in business ethics, utilitarianism, egoism is utterly mistaken. For I should be concerned not with my own self-interest or happiness, but with that of everyone. I should be entirely impartial between my own interest and that of others, putting my own interests into the scale along with everyone else's, even at very great cost to myself. Utilitarianism is hard to believe. Whether a certain pleasure, or more strikingly perhaps, a pain, occurs within my life or someone else's is undoubtedly a matter that I should rationally be concerned about. Certainly no human being has ever behaved as if the difference between their own life and that of others was of no significance.

But egoism is equally hard to believe. Imagine that you work as an accountant for a large company which imports goods from the developing world. Under your contract, you are required to pay a very large amount to a certain medium-sized company in the Sudan by 1 August. It is now 2 July. You know that payment now will enable this company to survive, thus vastly improving the prospects of the well-being of its employees. The money is already in a payment account, where it is not gathering interest for your own company. Surely you have *some* reason, even if it is only a weak one, to send the cheque now rather than later? Once it is accepted that people can have some reason to offer great services to others at no cost to themselves, egoism is no longer an option, since it suggests that all reasons are self-interested. And once other-regarding reasons are accepted, it is hard to see why they should not trump self-interested reasons in certain cases. Imagine that sending the cheque now will require your walking across the road to a post-box, and it is a cold day. Is this enough to make your not sending the cheque rational or reasonable?

A complete denial of the force of moral principles, then, is implausible. It may be that moral principles in business have little force against the rationality of self-interest, of course, but that is a question to be decided within philosophical business ethics itself.

Another sceptical line of argument involves pointing out how the moral principles accepted in various societies now and in the past to govern business have varied wildly. Compare, for example, attitudes in modern developed countries towards child labour with those of a century or so ago in those same countries, or with those which now exist in certain less developed countries. Does this huge variation in ethical view not suggest that there is no truth to be had in this area, and that moral principles are merely expressions of particular largely culturally determined attitudes?

One response here might be to claim that there is more homogeneity in moral belief than is often thought. But this response is less successful than one which accepts the possibility of huge variation in ethical belief but denies that this shows anything much about the status of moral principles themselves. Imagine two people looking at a light, one saying that it is red and the other that it is green. We have a puzzle on our hands, but it is easy to solve, since one person is colour-blind. Similarly, we shall often be able to explain differences in moral view using sociological, anthropological, cultural, and other data. For example, views about child labour are often closely tied up with brute economic fact, or with views about the nature of children. Disagreement does not undermine the possibility of truth, in ethics as in science, though the defender of the possibility of truth should be prepared to say at least something about how errors arise. . . .

3.   THE ABSTRACTNESS OF PHILOSOPHY

The arguments against business ethics I discussed in the previous section were general arguments against any kind of ethics, and have usually been developed by philosophers. Another strand of objection to business ethics is a particular case of a more general objection to philosophy, especially moral philosophy, as a whole, and it is often mounted, in the case of business ethics, by those engaged in business itself. According to this argument, philosophy's tools are ill-suited to deciding the everyday, practical, and contextually rich ethical questions which arise in business. Philosophers are trained in thinking about philosophy, and this is a discipline governed by universal and general modes of theoretical enquiry, which have little to offer the person seeking to deal with a real-life problem in business ethics, with all its messy particularities. "You have to be there," the philosopher is told.

There are at least two responses to this point about abstractness. The first is that the gap between philosophy and real life is not as great as the objector implies. One way to deal with a real moral problem is unthinkingly to do whatever you feel like doing at the time, and some people of course do exactly this. But most people stop to think, and when they do so they are doing moral philosophy, that is, seeking to provide the course of action they eventually choose with some kind of universal justification. A high-ranking employee of a multinational is asked to supply what appear to be bribes to an official in another country to secure a contract. "What if everybody did that?" he or she thinks. This is one of the fundamental questions underlying Kantian ethics. Then, "But everybody *is* doing this, so maybe it's not so bad after all. Still, wouldn't it do some good for a corporation as large and influential as ours openly to distance ourselves from such practices?" The idea that what we do should do some good is the thought animating consequentialist and utilitarian theories of ethics. And finally: "But I just don't want to be the kind of person who gets messed up in dubious and possibly unjust practices like this, whatever the consequences." These thoughts sit well with forms of virtue ethics influenced by Aristotle. And this list goes on. It is not as if our everyday moral thinking has arisen from nothing; it has emerged from those very traditions that lie behind contemporary moral theory.

The second response to the abstractness objection is to concede something to the objector. Philosophy, including moral philosophy, can be abstract, in that it consists in the articulation of rather general principles, with wide application, which require much interpretation if they are to serve as guides for everyday life. And if they are going to be applied to everyday problems of business ethics, whether in real life or in the pages of business ethics journals, this will require some understanding of those problems themselves. Consider, for example, the question of leveraged buyouts (LBOs). In the 1980s, some major U.S. corporations contracted debts of unprecedented proportions. Almost no one will deny that there was (indeed is) *some* risk of this leading to serious economic problems in future, affecting the well-being of many thousands of people. Now there is an empirical question about the level of risk here, and of course that will require a proper grasp of the nature of LBOs. This question is independent of the ethical question of whether LBOs are morally acceptable, in that it can be answered independently of that ethical question. But the ethical question cannot be answered independently of the empirical question. A philosopher who is going to write about business ethics needs to know about business, at least that area of business about which he or she is making claims. This, I suggest, is one reason why case studies are so important in the teaching of business ethics. Business ethics case studies teach us about business as well as about ethics.

There is here a general point to be made about the nature of applied, practical, or normative ethics. Applied ethics, including business ethics, comes under criticism on two fronts. Those involved in the practice itself say that philosophy is too abstract to be of serious help, while some philosophers say that philosophy should deal only with the universal and leave the practical to those who understand it. But, as I have argued, this dichotomy between theory and practice is a mistake. Most of those engaged in business will think through some ethical issue at some stage in their career, and philosophy here can be of great help in suggesting lines of thought, opening up logical possibilities, or extending the imagination. But it must be philosophy grounded in an understanding of practice. Business ethics, as a philosophical discipline, has its own independent and important role in our society.

It is worth noting here the interesting fact that philosophical business ethics tends to meet with more raised eyebrows than philosophical medical ethics. This is, I suspect, because of the fact that our commonsense morality is deeply concerned with matters of life and death, and these are of course at the heart of medicine. Those involved in medicine realize this, and most are already thinking ethically and are ready to welcome any assistance philosophy can provide. Business, on the face of it, is not a matter of life and death, and its practitioners do not traditionally go in for much ethical thinking. But this attitude is mistaken, for two reasons. First, our commonsense morality may be mistaken. It may be, that is, that business is as challenging ethically as medicine. Secondly, business *is* a matter of life and death. Business interests maintain the world order: the distribution of goods, with all the pleasures and pains it brings along with it, is a matter of business; and the future of the world depends on the way business responds to the environmental crisis. And, of course, business affects people's lives in less dramatic ways all the time. . . .

4. PHILOSOPHY AS AN IDLE WHEEL

Another objection to philosophy, closely related to the abstractness objection, is based on claims not so much about the general nature of philosophy as about its place in our society. This objection suggests that philosophy has turned itself into a highly specialized discipline, and that its methods and style have led to its moving out of the public arena entirely and retreating to the universities. Business people, not necessarily because philosophy is too abstract (though this may of course be so) but because it is just too difficult to understand in its contemporary form, largely ignore philosophical business ethics. Meanwhile, though some philosophers clearly do have a deep understanding of business, they use this knowledge to develop arguments in journals and books for their colleagues, and do not trouble themselves to communicate with those really concerned with the ethics of business. Philosophers might as well concern themselves with the ethics of feeding Christians to the lions or the ethics of time-travel: all they use business for is as a source of interesting problems, and history and the imagination could supply them with what they want just as efficiently as does real life.

There are several responses to make on behalf of philosophy here. First, let us for the sake of argument accept the main point of this objection. Let us assume, that is, that philosophical business ethics has made itself out of touch, through its excessive use of jargon and technicality. Even if this is true of contemporary business ethics, it is not true of Plato, Aristotle, and most of the other great writers in the history of moral philosophy. Anyone could read their works and consider their implications for the way they live.

Secondly, however, we should note that this objection exaggerates in two ways. Not all contemporary business ethics is comprehensible only to practitioners of business ethics as a discipline. Indeed, I would argue that most of what is currently published in philosophical business ethics is accessible to most moderately intelligent business people (its quality, of course, is another matter). Nor is it correct that business people ignore philosophical business ethics; they themselves publish in the area, many business schools teach courses in philosophical business ethics, and conferences and meetings on business ethics—at least those I have attended—always include at least some business people. Though it might be unfair even to suggest this, it might be the case that any apparent standoff that exists between contemporary business ethics and business itself is at least as much the fault of the majority of business people, who do not take the trouble to discover even the basics of philosophical business ethics, as it is of over-technical philosophers.

It has to be admitted, however, that some of the most important writings on business ethics can become quite complex, and require some grounding in philosophy for them to be understood. And if, as I have suggested, philosophical business ethics is seamlessly woven into philosophical ethics itself, we should admit that some contemporary ethical theory, with its talk of agent-relativity and agent-neutrality, for example, is quite complicated. But difficult questions are likely to require difficult answers, so a certain level of complexity is only to be expected. Sometimes, of course, philosophical technicality, formalization, and jargon are unnecessary, being added either because the author has forgotten the importance of communication to a wide audience in this area or because he or she is attempting to add a veneer of quality to an argument which may in fact be quite simplistic, vague, or implausible. But sometimes they are necessary. And here there is a task for the philosophical translators, those who are able to take the difficult concepts and arguments from contemporary discussion and translate them into ideas which can be grasped by and may be of use to business people who are seeking ethical understanding of their own lives.

Business people should be encouraged to think philosophically by any means at our disposal, whether it be through philosophical translation in generalist business journals and papers, or through education at business school. Such education is itself part of moral education in general, and there is here a substantive point to be made about the relation between philosophical principle and everyday practice. Early in his *Ethics*, Aristotle tells us that you will become a better person not just by attending his lectures. That requires that you have been brought up or habituated in the right way by your parents, school, or whatever. You need some basic grip on ethics and its problems before philosophical reflection and principle can help. Education in philosophical business ethics is part of the moral education of business people in general. Again, we can see a role for case studies, which sensitize those who study them to the salient features of cases of a kind which is likely to reoccur in real life.

5. ENDLESS DISAGREEMENT

In section 2 above we saw how the fact of disagreement between cultures is sometimes used by philosophers to suggest that there is no truth to be had in ethics. The fact of disagreement, however, can be turned against philosophy itself. We saw how disagreement is consistent with there being a truth, so the argument that disagreements among philosophers in business ethics suggest that there is no truth to be had will not succeed. But philosophers in business ethics do, of course, disagree greatly with one another, at every level, from that of general theory to its application to very specific cases. How, then, it might be asked, can they provide any guidance to business people? Of course, as a business person, I can go to philosopher P and ask for advice, and he will tell me to do X. But why should I listen to P when his or her colleague down the hall, Q, would give me philosophical arguments for doing not-X? Until philosophers can agree, they should not consider themselves entitled to offer advice they can be confident of.

It is important to recognize first that there is in fact a great deal of agreement in philosophical business ethics. Most philosophers in the area will agree that morality requires business people to respect the principle of client confidentiality, to pay debts, to ensure that any product is reasonably safe before releasing it onto the market, to pollute the environment as little as possible, and so on (this will be a very long list).

But, surely, it will be said, this is just to play into the hands of the objector. For if everyone agrees that something is right or wrong, why do we need philosophers? After all, it is not only philosophers who think that morality requires the things mentioned above. Here we can learn again from Aristotle's discussion of moral education. According to Aristotle, the person who starts thinking seriously about ethics should know "the that," that is, should have the basic grasp of ethics I mentioned when discussing Aristotle in the previous section. The student at business school who quite sincerely thinks that it is an entirely open question whether to repay a debt, or whether to remove competitors by taking out contracts on them, is unlikely to learn much from Business Ethics 101. But knowing the that is not enough for the ethical life; one must also have some understanding of "the because," of the reasons which lie behind one's ethical beliefs. Here, philosophy—including business ethics as it is taught in the business schools—can help.

Why should I repay a debt? Because it is unfair not to do so and violates the principle of respect for persons; because not doing so may have bad consequences; because it is dishonest. Or so proponents of Kantianism, utilitarianism, and virtue ethics, respectively, will tell us. But here again it may be said that I am playing into the hands of the objector. I have claimed that there is much agreement in business ethics, but in fact this agreement about the conclusions of certain arguments masks yet more fundamental disagreement about the premises of those arguments. Why should I listen to the utilitarian, when the Kantian has arguments just as good and which have persuaded many serious thinkers? But then why should I listen to the Kantian, when I see that the same can be said of virtue ethics?

Even at the theoretical level, however, disagreement is not as deep as the proponents of various ethical theories might suggest. Much contemporary moral philosophy, business ethics included, operates on a mistaken scientific model. If we are seeking to explain some phenomenon scientifically, only one of several competing theories can be accepted. But business ethics is not seeking to explain, but to justify. It is seeking those principles or reasons which should govern our actions. Here, most philosophers have been tempted to think that you have to nail your colours to a particular mast, picking one theory to justify a particular course of action. But reasons do not operate like this, since it is an obvious fact of everyday life that one can have more than one reason for doing something. If I say, "I am going to the opera because I want to see my cousin sing," it would be absurd for you to conclude that therefore I am not going in order to enjoy the music. I might be going for both reasons. Why is it, then, that philosophers have not noticed that it is equally absurd to suggest that if you think it is wrong not to pay a debt because it violates a principle of respect for persons, you cannot think that it is wrong because of its consequences or because it is dishonest? In other words, you do not have to choose a single ethical theory and stick with it; you can take what seems most plausible from several theories and seek insights from all of them.

There are, of course, going to be instances—such as the question of the nature of the person, or of the weight of self-interest against morality—where genuine, deep, and fundamental disagreement persists. Here each reasonable person will want to make up his or her own mind in the light of the best evidence available. Part of that evidence, perhaps most of it, will be the various competing arguments available in the various philosophical traditions.

These disagreements at the theoretical level are a large part of what explains the fact that there is a great deal of practical disagreement in business ethics on certain issues. At one end of the spectrum is the non-payment of debt or the murder of competitors: these are pretty well universally condemned. But on many other topics in business ethics there is a great deal of serious disagreement. What, for example, is the nature of the corporation, and can it have responsibilities or obligations? Does company loyalty speak against whistle blowing? Is persuasive advertising immoral?

A strong objector to philosophical business ethics may here advocate that business people ignore philosophers until they can come to some consensus on, say, the nature of the person and its ethical implications. Until that time, listening to the arguments of any one philosopher will be largely a waste of time, since other philosophers will have quite different arguments which, the philosophical experts will agree, are to be taken equally seriously. If one insists on having a view here, one might as well just toss a coin, or rather several coins, and adopt one's views according to chance.

But this objection is highly misguided, and for several reasons. First, philosophy cannot be opted out of in this way. As I have already pointed out, everyday thought is on a continuum with the most abstract philosophy, and behind everyday decision making will lie certain everyday assumptions about the nature of persons and the demands of morality. As David Wiggins has put it, harking back to a point of C. S. Peirce, "If someone says he dispenses with all metaphysics and wants none, you will be wise to expect him to be bogged down in a metaphysic so poor that, if it were explicitly revealed, you would not know whether to laugh or cry."

Secondly, even if there is disagreement at a high philosophical level about these fundamental ethical and metaphysical issues, there may be agreement among philosophers at a lower level about what sorts of view are untenable, or the undesirable implications that follow from certain views. Consider, for example, Ivan Boesky's tee-

shirt aphorism, that "He who owns the most when he dies, wins."
Most philosophers could quickly point out at least two serious problems with this claim. First, it is hard to understand even in its own
terms. If I live my life in such a way that I am very poor throughout,
so that I can inherit a vast amount on my deathbed, it is not clear
that I have made the right decision. Secondly, ownership itself, as
Aristotle saw long ago, does not seem to be a good in itself. Owning
property is merely a means to things which are goods in themselves.
Of course, Boesky could modify his view to deal with these points.
But then he would be doing philosophy.

Finally, the global benefits flowing from reflective attitudes must
be considered. Imagine that an analogue of the strong objection had
been accepted before the Scientific Revolution: clever scientists have
been studying these problems for a long time, it might have been
said, and they cannot agree, so we might as well give up. Science,
through the working out of the fundamental disagreements of its
practitioners, made the huge advances which lie behind the whole
shape of the modern world. There is no good reason to think that
philosophy is not capable of the same advances. This is to say that
philosophical business ethics, if it is pursued vigorously and consci-
entiously by philosophers and business people, may make advances
in ethical thinking on which there will be consensus in the future. We
can hypothesize that business would be run on more moral lines if
this were the case, and this is surely something to be welcomed. If it
is not welcomed, then we must return to the arguments of section 2
against scepticism.

The scientific analogy opens up a serious issue concerning why it
is that human beings do disagree about certain fundamental issues. In
the case of science, the explanation was often belief in fundamental-
ist religion. Now, even most of those committed to the forms of religion which have emerged from this fundamentalism will admit that
in previous centuries certain religious beliefs distorted people's vision
when it came to scientific matters. Why is it that some philosophers
now are committed utilitarians, while others are committed Kantians,
virtue theorists, or holders of some yet other view? This is a question
surprisingly little discussed in contemporary philosophy. But it is not
just something that happens without explanation; there must be a reason. And if there is a truth in ethics, which one of these views has cap-

tured, or which none of them has, or which each of them has in part, then the probability is that some philosophers are being led astray by certain mistaken fundamental metaphysical or ethical assumptions.

This raises the further question of the ideal conditions for approaching truth in ethics, whether ethics in general or business ethics. These ideal conditions, I suggest, are somewhat similar to those in science: intelligence and impartiality on the part of the enquirer, and the necessary resources for enquiry. Some scientists make discoveries on their own. But many scientists in the past and present have made their discoveries only through discussing their views in free and open discussion with others. That is particularly important in philosophy, and indeed in business ethics. Shutting down channels of communication, from either end, between philosophers and business people can only impede the search for truth.

6. IMMORAL ETHICS?

. . . The final objection to business ethics, though it comes from within philosophical ethics itself, is closely related to that discussed at the end of the previous section. Here, a proponent of a particular view in philosophical ethics will castigate the proponents of some other view for leading people away from the true path. Utilitarians have come in particularly for this sort of criticism in recent decades, the idea being that somehow they are likely not only to mislead people philosophically, but to corrupt them in some way.

But intellectual and practical toleration are essential if progress is to be made in ethics. Business ethicists, like all philosophers, indeed all reflective human beings, require a split mind. On the one hand, they may adhere to certain views about fundamental issues concerning the nature of the world, the nature of persons, and ethics, and views about the implications of these positions for issues of practical import in business. But, on the other hand, they must recognize that the disagreements that exist between equally serious, impartial, and reflective enquirers make it rather unlikely that they themselves are in possession of the full truth. At this point, they should accept that the practice of reflective enquiry, in business ethics as elsewhere, must be encouraged through openness, and not stifled by those with closed minds.

REVIEW AND DISCUSSION QUESTIONS

1. Do you agree with Crisp that egoism provides an implausible account of right and wrong? Is it true that other-regarding reasons can sometimes trump self-interested reasons?
2. Does the fact that now and in the past different societies have upheld very different ethical standards imply that we must be ethical relativists? Explain why or why not. When non-philosophers discuss ethics, they often gravitate toward ethical relativism. Why do you think this happens?
3. Some critics complain that contemporary business ethics is too technical and full of jargon. Do you see this as a serious problem? What about the charge that business ethics can provide little guidance because philosophers writing about it disagree among themselves?
4. Crisp concedes that there is serious disagreement about many topics in business ethics. Assess his three responses to the objector who contends that businesspeople should ignore philosophers until they can reach some consensus about these matters. Do you find them persuasive?
5. Do you agree that philosophical business ethics is important? Should businesspeople be encouraged to think about philosophical issues? Are there any problems or criticisms of business ethics that Crisp has ignored or failed to do justice to? In your view what are the main tasks of business ethics, and what challenges does it face?

SUGGESTIONS FOR FURTHER READING

General introductions to business ethics are provided by Richard T. De George, *Business Ethics*, 5th ed. (Prentice-Hall 1999), Manuel Velasquez, *Business Ethics*, 5th ed. (Prentice-Hall 2001), and William H. Shaw, *Business Ethics*, 4th ed. (Wadsworth 2002). For discussions of the nature and value of business ethics from different perspectives, see A. Stark, "What's the Matter with Business Ethics?" *Harvard Business Review* 73 (May–June 1993); William H. Shaw, "Business Ethics Today: A Survey," *Journal of Business Ethics* 15 (May 1996); J. Angelo Corlett, "A Marxist Approach to Business Ethics," *Journal of Business Ethics* 17 (January 1998); and Norman Bowie, "Business Ethics, Philosophy, and the Next 25 Years," *Business Ethics Quarterly* 18 (January 2000). Three good sources of advanced work in business ethics are the *Business and Professional Ethics Journal, Business Ethics Quarterly*, and the *Journal of Business Ethics;* see also Alan Malachowski, ed., *Business Ethics: Critical Perspectives on Business and Management*, 4 vols. (Routledge 2001).

CHAPTER TWO

The Responsibilities of a Businessman

J. R. Lucas

In this essay, J. R. Lucas, formerly Reader in Philosophy and Fellow of Merton College, Oxford, argues that men and women in business have ethical obligations that go beyond merely maximizing profits and obeying the law. Businesspeople almost always have some scope for decision making, and they do not act irrationally by taking into consideration other concerns besides immediate profits and staying within the law. Lucas goes on to identify the obligations that businesspeople have, which arise from the nature of business and the role it plays in our society. In particular, he looks at business's relationships to its shareholders, to its employees, to customers and suppliers, to competitors, and to the community, and the responsibilities that these relationships create.

THINGS TO CONSIDER

1. Lucas rejects the idea that it is irrational for a businessperson to do anything but try to maximize profits. Why?
2. Some businesspeople are skeptical about the idea that they have any obligations other than the pursuit of profit, but Lucas writes that their skepticism is "selective." Explain what he means.
3. What does Lucas have in mind when he writes, "cooperation, not competition, is the most fundamental aspect of business"?
4. C. B. Handy identifies six different "stakeholders" to whom a business can have obligations. What are they? What does Lucas add to this list?
5. Why does Lucas believe that "shareholders do not own their company"?
6. Lucas believes that a business can have obligations to its competitors. What does he have in mind?

Reprinted by permission from Christopher Cowton and Roger Crisp, eds., *Business Ethics: Perspectives on the Practice of Theory* (Oxford: Oxford University Press, 1998).

7. At the end of his essay, Lucas writes that businesspeople are often victims of "false images" that they have about themselves. What does he mean?

I

Many thinkers deny the possibility of businessmen having responsibilities or ethical obligations. A businessman has no alternative, in view of the competition of the marketplace, to do anything other than buy at the cheapest and sell at the dearest price he can. In any case, it would be irrational–if, indeed, it were possible–not to do so. Admittedly, there is a framework of law within which he has to operate, but that is all, and so long as he keeps the law he is free to maximize his profits without being constrained by any moral or social considerations, or any further sense of responsibility for what he does.

This view is mistaken. Economic determinism is false. The iron laws of supply and demand are not made of iron, and indicate tendencies only, without fixing everything, leaving no room for choice. In economic affairs we are often faced with decisions, and often can choose between a number of alternative courses of action. It is up to us what we do; we are responsible agents, and may fairly be asked to explain why we did as we did.

Nor do canons of rationality pick out one single course of action as the only rational one to take. They do not show that it is irrational to do anything other than maximize our profits. It is a mistake to construe rationality in terms of maximizing. Even though some economists, influenced by the Theory of Games, offer it as a definition, it is, as the prisoners' dilemma shows, an incoherent one. For individuals each to seek to maximize their own payoff can lead to sub-optimal outcomes assessed in maximizing terms. It may seem like a good idea for me to maximize irrespective of what others do, but if it is really a good idea for me, it is a good idea for them too, and then we shall all be worse off than if we had each pursued a policy that considered others as well as ourself. Rationality requires us not just to maximize, but also to widen our range of concern. We accept that it would be foolish to be guided only by immediate payoffs without considering future ones; we need to extend our vision not only over times, but over persons, identifying with certain groups, and thinking not only of my individual good, but our collective one as well.

It is a mistake, finally, to think that once the law has been laid down, the businessman is free to pursue profits within the limits laid down by law. The standards enforced by the law can only be minimal ones, not replacing moral standards, but needing to be supplemented by them. We generally acknowledge that there is a moral obligation to obey the law, and that almost every legal system enshrines much moral teaching, and that moral considerations have an important influence on the interpretation and development of the law. The legal system would break down unless most people obeyed most laws most of the time, and unless witnesses told the truth, and judges and juries reached honest verdicts, without being made to by the threat of coercion. We need the law to be enforced on occasion because civil society, unlike some voluntary associations, is unselective, and contains some members who are not minded to abide by the law, and would flout it if they could; and if they got away with it, others would follow suit. The law therefore needs to be backed by the threat of coercive sanctions, but just because these sanctions are severe, their use has to be subject to many safeguards. We need trials and burdens of proof, and often are chary about legislating against some admitted evil on account of the difficulty of actually enforcing the law, or of the dangers of blackmail, or for many other cogent reasons. Hence the standard required by the law is necessarily a minimal one, well below what is tolerable in social or commercial life.

Businessmen do have some, although only limited, room for making decisions; they are not being irrational if they take into consideration a wider range of concerns than simply maximizing immediate individual profit; and their legal duties do not exhaust their obligations generally. In deciding what to do, and justifying their decisions afterwards, there are a variety of reasons, for and against, the different courses of action open to them, these reasons not being necessarily confined to maximizing profits while keeping within the law.

. . . Corporations have no souls: they cannot be called to witness to artistic integrity, the monastic ideal, or altruistic devotion to another's good. But it does not follow that the ordinary universal obligations of communal life do not apply to them. These obligations arise from the activities we engage in and the context in which we carry them out, and apply to businesses as much as to other undertakings not because they have souls, but because they are centres of decision taking.

It would still be possible for a businessman to remain sceptical. Scepticism is always possible—at a price. The tough-minded can dismiss all concern for the environment as unrealistic woolly-mindedness, and may defer payment to his suppliers until the last possible moment: but when the Mafia call, and suggest that he might like to purchase protection from arson attacks, he is likely to be indignant. He believes vehemently in the rule of law, and that violence has no place in a civilized society; his scepticism, in short, is selective. And each selection of sceptical theses is likely to turn out incoherent. Different arguments are needed to show the untenability of different positions, and with each position there is a contrast between immediate self-interest, narrowly conceived, and wider-ranging reason, conveniently termed moral. Morality and self-interest remain opposed, but each version of self-interest is seen ultimately to be lacking in enlightenment. Scepticism is always possible, but never in the long run reasonable.

II

The positive grounds of obligation for a businessman arise from the nature of business. Contrary to present perceptions, business is fundamentally a cooperative activity. Business transactions would not take place unless there were fruits of cooperation that could, perhaps by means of some pecuniary adjustment, benefit both parties. Business transactions are essentially two-sided, with both parties benefiting as the result of the transaction. Cooperation, not competition, is the most fundamental aspect of business, and though competition remains important, the cooperative setting constitutes grounds for many obligations which a businessman should recognize. Moreover, the cooperation is normally long term and wide-ranging; the one-off transaction is the exception rather than the rule. Business is typically a process continuing over time and set within a definite social system of mutual understanding. I sell to customers who are in the habit of buying the sort of goods I sell, and buy from suppliers, who make their living by regularly and reliably supplying goods or services to those who want them. The obligations of a businessman arise from the cooperative nature of business, and the shared values and mutual understanding of the cooperative associations within which business transactions take place.

In many cases the cooperative setting is obvious. It is only because shareholders, superiors, colleagues, and employees cooperate with him that a businessman is able to do business, and the shared values on which that cooperation is based constitute considerations he should have in mind when reaching his decisions. Exactly what duties he has to shareholders, superiors, colleagues, and employees, and, more problematically, how conflicts of duties are to be resolved, still remains to be seen. But it is hardly controversial to claim that he does have duties to them, and that these duties arise from their being fellow members of the same business enterprise. It is, however, controversial to argue that a businessman has duties also to his customers, suppliers—and even his competitors—for in these cases we are more immediately aware of the adversarial, competitive aspect of the relationship, which seems altogether external. And, indeed, these relationships *are* more external. There *is* an adversarial element in bargaining with suppliers or customers, and competitors *are* competing. But bargains cannot take place unless there is some cooperators' surplus to bargain about, and nobody will do business with me in order to make me better off. Only if I hold myself out as meeting the other person's wants or needs will that person want to do business with me, so that if I am a person people want to do business with, I must see myself as others see me, and see to it that my business is good from their point of view. Although I may, for a season, be successful in ripping customers off, I cannot construct a coherent account of what I do in those terms alone, as I cannot offer any reason why people should want to do business with me. Much as we distinguish what it is to be a good doctor from what it is to be a successful one, so we can, following Plato's lead in the first book of the *Republic,* argue that the role of the businessman is socially defined in terms of the services he offers to others. These provide the criteria for judging whether he performs his role well or ill, and constitute grounds for his obligations to those he does business with. My competitors share these, and we collectively may need to uphold standards, and ensure that the public is well served by members of our trade generally. Beyond these shared values, there is the further bond of a common humanity, which enjoins us to recognize other people as fellow human beings; so that even where I have no common interest with my customers, suppliers, or competitors, I still need to treat them as persons, each with his own point of view, to whom I have, as a matter of justice, certain obligations of fair dealing and honesty.

III

C. B. Handy distinguishes six different sorts of "stakeholder," whose interests ought to be considered by those taking decisions: financiers, employees, suppliers, customers, the environment, and society as a whole; he argues that these six classes constitute a hexagon, within which a decision maker has to balance different, and sometimes conflicting, obligations (Handy 1995: 130–31, 143). Further distinctions may be drawn. Shareholders are in a different position from other creditors. Employees have obligations to employers, as well as vice versa. Obligations to society comprise obligations to the local community, to the nation and perhaps to the international community and the whole of mankind. Many firms also recognize some obligation to their industry or trade. There are certain obligations of honesty and fair play to competitors. We may summarize:

1. shareholders
2. employees and employers
3. customers
4. suppliers
5. creditors
6. competitors
7. trade or profession
8. the local community
9. the state
10. the international community and mankind generally
11. the environment

It is tempting to describe these as duties. Certainly, we could tax a businessman to explain why he had failed to consider his shareholders, employees, locality, country, or the environment, and if the question were brushed off with a "Why should I? It is none of my business," his reply would sound hollow. But the word *duty* denotes a stringency of obligation that often does not obtain. The duties of avoiding violence and of honesty are stringent, but many obligations are *prima facie* only, and may be overridden by others. A business has to survive, and that may require sacking not just an incompetent, but even a hard-working, employee. Faced with the apparently insatiable demands of morality, a businessman may feel inclined to follow Machiavelli and relegate morality to a private world, as not being practicable in the serious conduct of affairs. That is a mistake. We can guard against that mistake by talking not of peremptory duties, but grounds of obligation. I do not always have to keep redundant or incompetent employees in work: but I have some obligation towards them. If the survival of the firm depends on it, I must take the hard decision: but I am not usually in that extremity, and may be able to postpone the sacking, giving warnings in the case of incompetence, and long notice in the case of redundancy. It is not a matter of hard-and-fast rules. A businessman is not required always to be soft. But neither need he be always ruthless as a matter of course.

Obligations to shareholders and employees, as well as obligations of shareholders and employees, are primarily internal obligations, arising out of shared concerns. Obligations to customers, suppliers, creditors, and competitors are primarily external obligations, arising from our recognition of the validity of the other person's point of view as a necessary condition of making coherent sense of business activity. But in each of these cases some of the other considerations also apply, and the remainder are evidently mixed cases.

IV

It is often thought that public limited companies are owned by their shareholders, and that in consequence obligations towards shareholders are paramount. But, strictly speaking, shareholders do not own their company. Public limited companies are artificial creations, in which shareholders have certain rights, but as their liabilities are limited, so their rights are limited too. Their directors have certain specific obligations, spelled out by law, particularly in relation to takeover bids, and more generally to make the company prosper, but the latter does not override all other obligations. Managers are not under an obligation to drive the hardest bargain possible on each and every occasion so as to maximize dividend payments. Although they have a commission to seek profits, they have, as in all cases of people acting on behalf of others, some discretion as to how they carry out their commission, and are empowered to take other factors into consideration. Paying employees more may mean less money immediately available for dividends, but may prove more profitable in the long run, and may also enhance the standing of the company. Although the shareholders might instruct their board to go for immediate profits and to screw their employees as much as possible, it is not to be assumed as a matter of course that shareholders want to be Gradgrinds. The natural assumption is that they want their company to be one they can be proud of, treating its employees fairly and doing its bit for the locality in which it operates and the wider context in which it carries on business. It is a matter of degree: Pilkington, an exceptionally generous and community-minded firm, gave just over 0.4 per cent of its profits in charitable donations in 1983 (Sorell and Hendry 1994: 160). Only the most exacting shareholders could insist on their dividends being increased by a negligible amount rather than their company play its part in its sphere of operations.

Shareholders have duties. Some are spelled out by law—mostly concerned with treating other shareholders fairly if acquiring a majority of the shares. Others arise from the fact that each shareholder derives some benefit from the operations of his company, and can make his voice heard at the annual general meeting. Many modern thinkers deny that shareholders are under any obligations—their motive for buying shares is to make money, and that is their sole concern. But the argument is a *non sequitur:* there are many things I do in order to make money, but that does not abrogate my responsibilities in the matter. I may have invested money in land or houses, but am still open to criticism if the land becomes a public nuisance, or the houses are used for immoral purposes. Some pension funds have invested in works of art, but if the works of art went out of fashion and were consigned to the scrap heap, we should think that the fund had not only made a bad investment, but acted irresponsibly. Equally, if I own shares, I cannot escape from the obligations of ownership on the grounds that I had only owned them in order to make money. . . .

V

One reason why thinkers recently have been anxious to emphasize the duty of managers to maximize the shareholders' profit is that other competing claims have been advanced, and they fear that companies were coming to be regarded as milch cows to be run for the benefit of other parties, most notably of their employees. Businessmen do have obligations to employees, but not unlimited ones. The obligations arise from the common enterprise in which the employees engage to do what the employer tells them in return for a wage. There are two aspects to this relationship: not only the external, adversarial one in which their interests are opposed, but an internal, co-operative one, arising from the common enterprise that generates the surplus available for division between them.

The employer tells the employee what to do, and therefore shares responsibility for what he does. Both have responsibilities, but the employer has the greater one. He owes it to the employee to give him the amount of direction appropriate to the job, neither depriving him of all autonomy nor leaving him without clear objectives; and to ensure that he does nothing illegal, imprudent, or immoral. . . . Equally, the employee owes it to his employer to carry out instructions efficiently, and to exercise his discretion responsibly. . . .

Because the employer has greater responsibility, it is reasonable for him to shoulder greater burdens and have more of the benefits resulting from the enterprise. Although most contracts of employment are short-term, the reality is that most employment is fairly long-term. Employers could not train a new workforce each week, and employees value the security of a job. It is reasonable for the employer, in the absence of welfare provided by the state, to carry some of the risk of ill health, because the cost of an absentee is a small part of his budget, and can be averaged out over the whole of the workforce, whereas the loss of the weekly wage is calamitous for the individual; and in the same way, though both parties should give long notice, it is more incumbent on the employer to do so. But these obligations, though real, are not indefinitely extensible. Not only the idle and incompetent, but even the hard-working but redundant employee may have to be sacked, if the firm can no longer employ him profitably. It is not the employer's business to provide employment—and recent history makes it very doubtful whether it can be the state's responsibility either.

Many people think that employees should have a share of the profits, and that this would remove the adversarial element. It is a possible arrangement, adopted by a few firms, but it has difficulties. There is still an adversarial aspect in the determination of what share each employee should have. Moreover, profits are uncertain, and can well fail to materialize in bad years; few employees can withstand a prolonged drop in earnings. They are rationally risk-averse, and just as widows were encouraged to take preference shares with a lower but more reliable yield, so it is natural for employees to want a fixed return rather than a greater, but less certain, share in the profits. Again, the holders of tradable shares can be fairly relaxed about forgoing immediate dividends for the sake of future growth, whereas an employee approaching retirement, or thinking of moving jobs, has no incentive to support policies of ploughing back profits into the firm. These objections are none of them conclusive, but together suggest that the current practice of paying employees fixed wages rather than some share of the profits is a reasonable and fair one.

   In negotiating wages the employer's and employee's interests are opposed; but the immediate opposition is largely subsumed under a longer-term profitable partnership. It is in the interests of each that the other, and others similarly situated, should want to continue the relationship; and that therefore that it should be a profitable relationship from the other's point of view. These considerations do not suffice to determine an exact just wage or just price: usually we leave it to the market to determine the going rate, and normally to pay the going rate is fair enough. But the market is imperfect, and the market rate can be unfair; we can justly criticize the employer who pays starvation wages, even though he can find desperate workers ready to work for a pittance, and trade unions which drive industries into bankruptcy through their exorbitant wage demands.

VI

The relationship with customers and suppliers is much more external than that with shareholders or employees, and the obligations arise from the other-directedness of the business transaction rather than from a long-term association. Traditionally the responsibility has been on the purchaser to make sure that the transaction suits his purposes: *caveat emptor*, for only the purchaser can know what his priorities really are, and only he can decide whether to buy or not. But even in the Middle Ages there were qualifications of this doctrine. . . .

   It remains true that only the purchaser can decide what his priorities are, and that the final decision is his. But we now recognize that in deciding to buy he is not exercising an arbitrary whim in a particular case, but is to be presumed to be making a rational choice to buy some good or some service of a suitable type, whereupon the onus is on the seller, who is in a position to know what he has to sell, to supply what the purchaser may reasonably be supposed to want. *Caveat emptor* represents the ultimate responsibility of the unique individual who alone can decide what he shall do: *caveat vendor* the ensuing responsibility of the seller to meet the requirements of the sort of purchaser that someone who holds himself out as providing goods or services must expect to satisfy.

Those who sell get paid standardized units of accredited value. Since they can be sure that one man's money is as good as another's, they should be ready to treat all comers equally, and not discriminate against some or charge them extortionate prices. In some jurisdictions discounts may not be given at all, without prior permission, even to long-standing and valued customers, but usually discounts are allowed, provided the outsider is not greatly disadvantaged. Taxi drivers in St Petersburg or Prague, who charge exorbitant prices to vulnerable foreigners, are acting unfairly. If I can rely on being paid in standard coin of the realm, others should be able to rely on me to ask only standard charges for standard services.

Many modern businesses, some of them household names, cheat their suppliers by not paying them on time. It is thought to be clever financial management to defer payment until the last moment before a writ is issued, so as to increase cash balances or avoid paying interest on overdrafts. Many small firms have been bankrupted in consequence. The fact that the practice has not been effectively outlawed shows a shoddiness in British business culture of which all businessmen should be ashamed. Of course, it is open to a firm, and in some cases reasonable, to negotiate long terms of credit. The contract price will then reflect that fact. What is indefensible is to agree to pay at a certain time and then not pay. For the reasons already given, the law is difficult and expensive to invoke. The obligation is to pay on the date agreed, not when ordered to do so by a court. . . .

VII

It may seem strange to say that we have duties towards our competitors, because on the classical view we are locked in cut-throat competition with them in a zero-sum game, where their gain is our loss. But, as the analogy with games, competitions, and the law courts shows, the fact that the exercise is adversarial does not mean that there are no obligations, only that some do not obtain in these situations. The obligations of honesty and fair dealing hold good both in competitive sports and in the marketplace. Although there is a natural opposition of interest, with each party striving to succeed, even though it will be at the expense of its rivals, there are different ways of competing, and we have a strong intuitive sense of which are fair and which unfair. To provide a better product or render a better service at a lower price is fair: but when British Airways got hold of the names of those intending to fly with their rival, Virgin, and telephoned them offering a comparable flight at a reduced fare, it was properly seen as unethical conduct. They were not competing on a level playing field, but were using information they should not have obtained in order to make special offers, not open to the general public, to persuade just those who had made up their minds to fly with Virgin to change their minds. . . .

VIII

Firms have duties to the local community and to wider ones. The underlying argument is the one already given, that a firm is a corporation, a centre of decision making, and hence able, and needing, to take into account a wide variety of considerations in arriving at its decisions. In particular, a firm can reasonably be said to be located in the place where it operates. It has the power to alter the way things happen in its locality, just as I have in mine, and questions can be asked about the things it does, which a responsible businessman will want to be able to answer satisfactorily, and show thereby that business is, indeed, a cooperative exercise, and not merely a matter of self-interest. Three different sets of neighbours may be identified: the local community, the national state, and—perhaps—the whole of mankind. In addition, we can identify a non-personal neighbourhood, the environment, as being also a focus of concern. To a considerable extent the firm's responsibilities to the local community are commuted into the payment of rates and taxes. But sometimes there are special needs which the local community is unable to meet, or opportunities open only to the firm, and then there may be good reason for further action. As in other cases, the action can be justified on grounds of enlightened self-interest—if the locality is a good one and the local community flourishing, people will want to work for the firm and to do business with it—but in many cases the underlying motivation is purely moral.

Economic activities often pollute, and businessmen are often asked to take into consideration the effect they are having on the environment. Some feel obscurely guilty, and wonder if there is any way they can obtain a clean bill of health: others are robustly defiant, and say it is up to the legislators to lay down acceptable standards of emissions, and within those limits they are free to do whatever will maximize profits.

Both views are wrong. While it is true that all human activity impinges on the environment, it is not the case that it is necessarily for the worse. The English countryside is the result of centuries of human interaction with the land. Sometimes it is right to take steps to keep some areas in their pristine state: in Brazil almost all the Atlantic seaboard has been brought under cultivation, and it is right to protect the remaining virgin forest. The Amazon rainforest needs protection because of the extremely destructive exploitation to which it has been subject hitherto. But not every exploitation is malign: to eliminate malarial swamps or the very existence of the smallpox virus is to make the world a better place, even though a less natural one.

Many industrial processes, however, do have bad effects. Waste products pollute the atmosphere, the water table, or landfill sites. Each ton of coal burnt contributes to acid rain, eroding ancient buildings and destroying forests, and to the greenhouse effect, which may, for all we know, have disastrous consequences in the twenty-first century. Such considerations should weigh with anyone taking decisions. The view that it is up to the law to set limits to what may be legitimately done, and that within those limits the businessman is free to do whatever seems most profitable is, as we have seen, a mistake. The law is too crude an instrument to define accurately what may or may not be done, and often considerations of enforceability or public policy will make it impracticable or inexpedient to enact a law which, on the merits of the case, ought to be enacted. The fact that there is no law against sending out sulphur dioxide into the atmosphere is no reason for thinking that it is perfectly all right to do so. Considerations of practicality often also prevent laws actually in force from being enforced. Adverse neighbourhood effects are covered by the law of nuisance, but it is often difficult and expensive to invoke the law. Can an angling association prove in court that the dearth of fish in its stretch of the river is due to the effluent from my factory and not to that from another one higher up the stream? But the doctrine that one can damage one's neighbour so long as the damage cannot be provably laid at one's door is a doctrine that few responsible people would care to endorse.

The absence of legally enforced restraints is relevant. It determines the context in which the businessman operates, and the competition he has to meet. If everyone else is spewing out sulphur dioxide, I cannot afford to put in expensive apparatus to scrub my emissions—and anyhow it will not make much difference to an atmosphere already much polluted. My customers are not prepared to pay for the privilege of being environmentally pure, and the actual benefit will be marginal. And even if there were laws imposing strict controls on emissions, we should merely lose business to Third World countries that were not so pernickety.

There is force in these arguments, but they do not conclude the matter. At any one time we are caught up in a situation not of our own devising, and must live in the world as it is, not as we would like it to be. But we need not be completely conformed to the world. Some moves are open, at least to monitor, and perhaps to mitigate, the adverse effects of our activities. Carelessness, rather than economy, is often responsible for the worst pollution. Many effluents can be recycled, or made less noxious before they are released. Often, indeed, they can be degraded biologically, if only we allow time and take trouble to find the bacterium with the right appetite. And the pressure of the best practice is effective over time in raising standards in the locality, or industry, as a whole. . . .

IX

The considerations a businessman has to bear in mind are structured by the role he occupies as employee, colleague, manager, or director. He has duties to his superiors, to his directors, to his shareholders, which certainly restrict his freedom of action, and which may seem to leave him with no alternative. But often he is the victim of false images which distort the picture he forms of himself and his situation. He is led to believe that he has no freedom of action, or that his one overriding duty is to maximize the profits of the shareholders.

Yet he feels that the arguments are not all one way, and would like to be able to think clearly through a maze of conflicting responsibilities. It can be done, but is not easy. Often there is no clear-cut path of duty, and the businessman has to balance conflicting obligations. But that is nothing new. We are familiar with the dilemmas of private life, and though their resolution is not easy, we are sometimes able to discern what we ought to do. The same is true in business life. If we can understand, without distortion, the true nature of business trans-actions, we can try to think out the differing obligations that flow from them. The aim of this article is to help the businessman do that; not to give him easy answers, but help him in the difficult task of working out his own answers on his own.

REFERENCES

Handy, C. B. (1995) *The Empty Raincoat* (London: Arrow Business).
Sorell, T., and J. Hendry. (1994) *Business Ethics* (Oxford: Butterworth-Heinemann).

REVIEW AND DISCUSSION QUESTIONS

1. Critically assess the widely held belief that the businessperson's only obligation is to maximize profits within the framework of the law.

2. Lucas writes that "business is fundamentally a cooperative activity" and that "the role of the businessman is socially defined in terms of the services he offers to others." Do you agree with these two propositions, and, if so, what are their implications for business ethics?

3. According to Lucas, businesspeople can have obligations to eleven different groups or things. Are some of the obligations Lucas identifies typically more important than others? Are there additional sources of obligation that should be added to his list? Should anything be dropped from the list?

4. For each of the categories that Lucas identifies, give an example of a specific obligation that a business might have.

5. Critically assess the idea that because the shareholders own the corporation, its obligations to them are paramount. Do you agree with Lucas that shareholders have duties? If so, what duties do they have?

6. What obligations do employers have to employees? What obligations do employees have to employers? Do employees have a right to a share of the profits?

7. In this essay, Lucas surveys the various responsibilities of business-people. Do you find his approach illuminating and helpful? Explain why or why not. Are there any issues or problems that he has over-looked, or are there any specific points of his that you disagree with?

SUGGESTIONS FOR FURTHER READING

In "The Social Responsibility of Business Is to Increase Its Profits," *New York Times Magazine,* September 13, 1970, Milton Friedman provides the classic statement of the position that Lucas argues against. There are many critical discussions of Friedman's ideas; one of the best is Thomas Carson, "Friedman's Theory of Corporate Social Responsibility," *Business and Professional Ethics Journal* 12 (Spring 1993). Kenneth E. Goodpaster, "Business Ethics and Stakeholder Analysis," *Business Ethics Quarterly* 1 (January 1991) discusses the obligations of managers to stockholders and other stakeholders. See also Rogene A. Buchholz and Sandra B. Rosenthal, "Social Responsibility and Business Ethics," in Robert E. Frederick, ed., *A Companion to Business Ethics* (Blackwell 1999), and Glenn Martin, "Once Again: Why Should Business Be Ethical?" *Business and Professional Ethics Journal* 17 (Winter 1998). Two useful essays on business ethics by distinguished economists are Kenneth J. Arrow, "Social Responsibility and Economic Efficiency," *Public Policy* 21 (Summer 1973), and Amartya Sen, "Does Business Ethics Make Economic Sense?" *Business Ethics Quarterly* 3 (January 1993).

CHAPTER THREE

The Ethics of Corporate Downsizing

John Orlando

In recent years, downsizing has become a major business trend. Although this trend may have improved the economy overall, its human price has been high as hard-working employees suffer the emotional and financial repercussions of losing their jobs. In this essay John Orlando, who teaches philosophy at Champlain College, Vermont, argues that downsizing is often morally wrong. He begins by challenging the assumption that the interests of shareholders take priority over those of employees, arguing instead for their moral equality. This equality implies that for downsizing to be permissible it must be justifiable from a utilitarian perspective, which takes into account the interests of both shareholders and workers. However, Orlando argues that the utilitarian case for downsizing is unproved and that there are at least three moral arguments against it. Although downsizing may be justified in extreme cases, for example, if it is necessary to save the corporation, Orlando concludes that downsizing merely to increase profit will usually be wrong.

THINGS TO CONSIDER

1. Orlando discusses six arguments intended to show that the interests of shareholders take priority over those of other groups. State each of those six arguments in one or two sentences.
2. Orlando argues that a utilitarian approach does not favor downsizing. Give one reason why not.
3. What is the "harming some to benefit others" argument against downsizing? What is the "legitimate expectations" argument?
4. Orlando's "fairness" argument against downsizing appeals to the idea that people should not be rewarded or punished for things for

From *Business Ethics Quarterly* 9 (April 1999). Copyright © 1999 The Society for Business Ethics. Reprinted by permission. Some notes omitted.

which they are not responsible. How does Orlando's example of
highly paid professional athletes illustrate that idea?

I. THE ISSUE

A survey of contemporary business ethics literature leads one to believe that the primary ethical questions facing businesses today concern topics such as affirmative action, sexual harassment, and the environment. While these are without a doubt weighty concerns, many
workers, especially manufacturing workers, would place corporate
downsizing—the closing of whole plants or divisions in order to increase profits—at the head of their list of ethically contentious
business practices. Though the issue has provoked considerable debate in the popular press, the philosophical community has largely
ignored it.

This oversight is curious given that downsizing is arguably the
major business trend of our era. . . . The statistics on downsizing's
human costs are sobering. One study found that 15 percent of downsized workers lost their homes, and another that the suicide rate
among laid-off workers is thirty times the national average.[1] Despite
the rosy picture of the economy painted by the popular media, where
attention is constantly drawn to the growth of the stock market, evidence suggests that trends such as downsizing have led to a general
decline in employee earnings, as well as a widening of the gulf between rich and poor in America.[2] Added to this is the fact that since
the loss of jobs is concentrated in a relatively small geographic area,
these closings affect the entire community. Businesses that rely upon
workers' spending will feel the pinch, often leading to secondary layoffs. Consequently, communities as a whole have been devastated by
such closings.[3] Downsizing also carries with it serious nonquantifi-
able harms. News of mass layoffs sends psychological tremors across
the nation, leading to general worker apprehension about job security and less job satisfaction.[4] Worse yet, the anxiety of unemployment often leads to psychological symptoms such as depression, or
expresses itself through a variety of unpleasant behaviors: i.e., crime,
domestic violence, child abuse, and alcohol and drug abuse.[5] . . .

I will argue that acts of downsizing are very often morally wrong.
I will begin by demonstrating that the business ethics literature has
yet to identify a morally relevant distinction between the situation of

the shareholder and that of the worker in relation to the corporation. This means that the corporate manager has no naturally greater duty to shareholders than to workers. I will make my case by examining, and dismissing, the various arguments advanced for privileging the interests of shareholders above all other parties. I then advance arguments against the moral permissibility of acts of downsizing. I will finish with a few words about how the concerns I raise might provide direction for future investigations into the ethical status of related practices, such as the replacement of full-time workers with part-time help.

II. The Moral Equality of Workers and Shareholders

Property Rights

First, it must be understood that one cannot justify the position that shareholder concerns take precedence over all other groups simply by appeal to the fact that the shareholders are the legal owners of the corporation. In that case, all one has done is provide a definition of the term *shareholder;* one has yet to provide a morally relevant reason for privileging the interests of that group. This is analogous to arguing that abortion is impermissible after viability because that is the point where the fetus could survive outside of the womb.

The natural tack at this point is to assert that a legal owner has property rights that allow her to dispose of her property in any manner she sees fit. But this justification skews the issue in the shareholder's favor by appealing to a paradigm that does not apply in the case of corporate ownership. The term *property rights* conjures up images of property for personal *use,* not *profit.* For instance, property rights advocates normally worry about laws that place restrictions on the use of one's homestead, such as laws regulating the appearance of one's home. Similarly, militia groups who dig in and take shots at ATF officials never barricade themselves in their businesses, but rather their homes. We may harbor a deep-seated intuition that property is sacred, but that intuition is tied to property with which we are in some respect intimately connected, such as a home.

To avoid glossing over the distinction between property for private use and property for profit, we will need to narrow our inquiry to an example of property for profit. Imagine that I own an apartment which I have rented to a couple for ten or fifteen years (think Fred and Ethel from "I Love Lucy"). I discover that I can make more money by dividing up the apartment and renting it to college students. My intuition is that I have a responsibility to the people who rent from me. At the very least, I should assure the couple, who might be frightened about the prospect of being thrown into the street, that I will not have them leave until they have procured similar housing elsewhere at a similar cost. I would also feel obligated to ensure that their transition is as easy as possible by, for instance, helping them move. Moreover, the purpose of the money will have a bearing on the moral status of the act. The act is far easier to justify if it is needed to pay for my wife's extended medical care, than if it merely allows me to buy a longer sailboat. Thus, the general appeal to property rights breaks down when the property in question is for profit, and when we turn to scenarios closer to the practice of downsizing itself.

Fiduciary Duties

Many theorists and business managers defend the moral superiority of shareholders on grounds that corporate managers are bound by a fiduciary duty to their shareholders that trumps any competing duties. The burden of proof is then taken to fall on the shoulders of those arguing against this position to demonstrate that the manager has equally strong duties to others as well. . . .

But this characterization of the issue misconstrues the lines of justification for the duties of an agent in a fiduciary relationship. The fiduciary duty does not establish the obligations of the agent; it is rather prior considerations pertaining to the nature of the relationship that determine the parameters of that duty. For instance, the fiduciary duty of a lawyer to her client is not the same as that of a realtor to his client. Thus, the fiduciary duty itself cannot establish the agent's obligations, since the obligations differ in the two cases. This means that we must look to the particularities of the relationship to identify the contours of the manager's duty to her shareholders. The term *fiduciary duty* is merely a label for whatever obligations the manager owes to the shareholder; it does not create those duties, and thus cannot justify them.

One important factor determining the nature of an agent's fiduciary duty is the reason why the principal requires the protection of that duty. That is, from what is the individual being protected? For example, much of the duty of a lawyer to her client involves not releasing information about the client to others. This can be justified on grounds that in order to mount an adequate defense, the client must feel free to speak candidly about his case. Thus, a lawyer's fiduciary duty to her client in criminal cases can be thought of as protecting the client from the state by ensuring the best possible defense. However, the fiduciary duty of the real estate broker is not of this sort, as here the protection is not from others, but rather from the real estate broker himself. The danger is that by knowing the seller's intentions and financial situation, a broker might collude with a potential buyer, or an agent acting on behalf of that buyer, to rig an offer for a quick commission. . . .

There is considerable evidence that the fiduciary duty of a corporate manager has been historically justified as a means of protecting the owner from that manager. The legal justification of this duty can be traced to the 1741 court ruling in *The Charitable Corporation v. Sir Robert Sutton*, where the court ruled that managers of corporations were "most properly agents of those who employ them." Interestingly, the suit was brought against the managers of The Charitable Corporation for "self-dealing by executives, theft, failure of inventory control, and a huge unmet financial commitment." Notice that the neglect of managerial duty cited involved not benevolent contributions to others, but rather acting in their *own* interest. . . .

Hence, there is good reason to believe that the legal basis of fiduciary duties of corporate managers to shareholders has been construed as the obligation to not advance their own interests against those of the shareholders. Adopting this view of the fiduciary relationship would mean that when a corporate manager takes into account the interests of stakeholders, even where that comes at the expense of profits, this does not conflict with a manager's fiduciary duty to shareholders.

Risk

Ian Maitland provides two justifications for the position that corporate managers have duties to shareholders over those to other parties. The first appeals to the fact that shareholders have invested capital in the corporation. Why is this fact morally relevant? According to Maitland, shareholders have taken a risk in placing their money in the hands of the corporation, and are thereby due compensation in the form of having their interests given privilege over those of other parties. Maitland states that:

> As a practical matter, no stakeholder is likely to agree to bear the risk associated with the corporation's activities unless it gets the commitment that the corporation will be managed for its benefit. That is logical because the stockholder alone stands to absorb any costs of mismanagement.[6]

It is strange, however, to think that the worker who loses his job has not absorbed any costs of mismanagement. Maitland's point must be that while workers stand to lose their jobs due to corporate mismanagement, they only lose future potential earnings, whereas shareholders lose something they have placed into the corporation. However, workers too have placed something at risk when accepting a job. At the very least, the worker has bypassed other possible job opportunities, opportunities that may have turned out to be financially more rewarding. Also, some have gone to school in the hopes of pursuing a career in the field, thereby investing substantial sums of money (or accruing substantial debt) in the process. Even more importantly, many workers have purchased homes in the expectation of a steady income, and in this manner have risked their homes on the corporation. We can also add to our list the various ways in which workers plant roots in the community which are disrupted when they are forced to relocate, such as placing their children in local schools or having their spouses accept jobs. While the worker's investment in a corporation is not of the same sort as the shareholder's, it constitutes a risk nevertheless, and so the worker's position is not dissimilar to that of the shareholder. The only difference between the risks taken by the two parties is one of degree, and the degree of that risk will depend upon the particular situation of each individual.

Contracts

Maitland's second argument is that corporations are fundamentally a "freely chosen . . . nexus . . . of contracts" between its stakeholders, which establish both the "rights" and the "obligations" of each party.[7] These contracts stipulate that the worker will give the corporation her labor in return for a fixed wage, while the shareholder will receive all of the profits of the corporation in return for investing capital in it. When third parties tinker with that arrangement, they violate the right of self-determination of the members of the contract, who have determined the terms of the contracts under "free," "voluntary," and "uncoerced" bargaining circumstances.[8]

But Maitland cannot possibly mean that such contracts are explicit, for no such document was signed by either shareholders or employees. He must therefore mean that some sort of implied contract exists between all parties involved. For example, as a teacher, I never explicitly state that I will not allow a student's membership in a morally repellent organization to bias the grades I give him, but this is certainly implied by the nature of our relationship.

However, Maitland's picture of the corporation simply does not square with reality. It turns out that most shareholders expect corporate managers to take into account the interests of other constituencies when making decisions about the welfare of the corporation.[9] More importantly, shareholders tend to think of themselves not as owners of the corporation, but rather as investors in it.[10] . . . For the vast majority of shareholders, dabbling in the stock market is thought of as one means among many of investing one's money, something chosen for its high rate of return, not in order to become a corporate owner. Thus, it is hard to understand how the investor can be acting under the assumption of an unstated contract between himself, management, and the company's employees. On the other side, employees have traditionally assumed that taking a job meant having it for life as long as they perform their duties well.[11] Given these considerations, if we are basing such contracts on the implicit understandings and expectations of the parties involved, the evidence actually points in the very opposite direction to which Maitland argues.

Finally, one can raise serious doubts about the assertion that the worker/manager/shareholder relationship has been established under "free, voluntary, and uncoerced" circumstances. For one, the parties are by no means in an equal bargaining position. Despite Maitland's insistence that the disgruntled employee can always "fire his boss by resigning,"[12] employees often find that they have very few job options given their skills, the labor market, and the costs of moving to another area. Shareholders, however, have thousands of companies from which to choose, and a variety of mechanisms specifically designed to make movement in and out of the stock market as easy as possible. . . .

Other People's Money

Milton Friedman also advances two arguments against the position that corporations have a responsibility to parties other than shareholders. Friedman's first objection is that "the corporation is an instrument of the stockholders who own it," meaning that the manager is acting with other people's money, and thus serving the public interest at the expense of profits is an impermissible use of that money.[13] Another way to put it is that any action that diminishes profits to aid other parties constitutes a "tax" on the shareholders' income.

However, such a use of the shareholders' income is only impermissible if it is unauthorized, and as I have noted, most shareholders expect managers to take into account considerations beyond maximizing profits. Moreover, shareholders in a modern corporation can withdraw their money from that corporation with a simple phone call, and thus the manager who announces his intention to act for the public good gives shareholders plenty of time to remove their money before such a "tax" is levied. More importantly, it is a generally accepted principle that moral duties "transfer through" from principal to agent, such that if it is morally forbidden for me to do something, then it is forbidden for me to enlist an agent to act on my behalf. Thus, an act of downsizing cannot be morally justified in virtue of the fact that it is done in the interests of the shareholders of the corporation, since if it is wrong for the shareholder to perform that act, then it is equally wrong for the manager to do so for them. The fact that a manager is an agent of others cannot itself make the action morally right, and therefore the moral status of the act will turn on other considerations.

Private vs. Public

Friedman's second objection is that requiring corporations to act in the social interest disrupts the private/public distinction which is at the heart of the free market system. Care for the public welfare, the objection goes, is properly the function of the state acting through officers specifically appointed for the task, not of businesspersons trained in other fields. Note that Friedman need not be against public welfare measures in principle, only those that place the burden of caring for the public welfare on the shoulders of corporations.

But this point can be met with at least two responses. First, one might argue . . . that corporations are best thought of as entities permitted to exist by the state because they serve the public good, not because individuals have a right to enrich themselves through them. Of course, corporate activities can end up doing both, but the issue concerns what justifies their existence, and in fact there is considerable historical evidence that corporations were originally conceived as a means of advancing the public good. Thus, the objection requires a defense of the position that corporations must only be run for the private good of their owners. Second, the objection cannot be applied to the case at hand. Downsizing concerns a corporation terminating the employment of its workers. Thus, unlike providing food and shelter to those in need, there is no public sector analogue to the service being demanded of corporations. . . .

I have argued that no philosophically sound argument has yet been advanced for privileging the interests of shareholders over those of workers simply by virtue of the fact that they are shareholders. This is not to say that no such argument may someday appear, but rather that in the absence of compelling reasons to the contrary, we must assume that the worker has an equal moral standing as the shareholder since they are, after all, both humans. Cast in this manner, the burden of proof in the debate runs contrary to what has been up to now believed by its participants. It has been tacitly assumed that it is the job of those arguing for the moral status of non-shareholders to establish their position, perhaps due to the earlier-mentioned view of fiduciary duties. But one of our most deeply felt convictions is that two human beings have equal moral status until morally relevant considerations can distinguish between them. Thus, it is really on the shoulders of those arguing for privileging the interests of the shareholders to make their case. This, I have argued, they have yet to do, leaving us to default to the presumption of equality.

The Utilitarian Argument

I now wish to examine the utilitarian defense of downsizing. It seems to me that once the moral equality of workers and shareholders has been granted, the only considerations that could justify acts of downsizing would be consequentialist in nature. At the very least, arguments currently advanced to justify acts of downsizing, when they do not rely upon the premise of a moral superiority of shareholders, have been utilitarian. Thus, if I can establish that the utilitarian case has yet to be made, I will have demonstrated that we have yet to find an adequate defense of downsizing.

. . . Utilitarianism is generally construed as the principle that the act that maximizes total utility is morally right. Thus, one could argue that downsizing benefits the majority of the population, and though it leaves some individuals by the wayside, the benefit to the whole outweighs the harm to the few. The entire economy, it might be argued, is becoming more efficient. Moreover, the stock market has skyrocketed, benefiting all those who have investments in mutual funds.

But there is reason to doubt whether downsizing has generated a net gain in utility. A group of researchers recently concluded a fifteen-year study which found that when acts of downsizing are not accompanied by careful restructuring of the corporation—in other words, when people are simply laid off in order to lower costs of production without thought of how the remaining employees will sustain levels of productivity—downsizing has always hurt the corporation in the long run.[14] Reich also notes that the downsizing trend has caused a general drop in employee loyalty in the United States.[15] Workers are far less likely to go the extra mile for firms who treat them as disposable cogs in the corporate machine. While loyalty is not easily quantifiable, and thus does not show up in a corporate ledger, it will affect the company's overall performance. . . .

But even if the case could be made that downsizing improves the overall health of the economy, there would still be a gap between this fact and the conclusion that overall utility has risen. If the argument were to terminate at this point, it would be assuming that one can equate well-being with financial gain; however, far more things go into determining one's well-being. For instance, it is indisputable that the anxiety from job loss has a profoundly negative influence upon one's psychic health. The harm of unemployment cannot simply be measured by the total loss of income; it produces fear for one's own well-being as well as the well-being of one's family, not to mention the anxiety experienced by those other groups themselves. When these factors are taken into account, it becomes clear that utilitarian considerations do not clearly point in favor of downsizing. It might in fact be determined that downsizing improves net utility in the long run, but the empirical evidence is inconclusive. Our position on the issue, therefore, will need to be informed by other considerations.

III. ARGUMENTS AGAINST DOWNSIZING

Harming Some to Benefit Others

Up to this point I have argued only that defenders of downsizing have failed to establish that downsizing is morally permissible. Here I will present reasons for thinking that downsizing is often morally wrong. The first argument appeals to the widely held intuition that it is wrong to subject individuals to certain types of harms in order to benefit others. Consider the following example: a town has recently experienced a rash of murders, such that people are afraid to go out at night, or concern themselves with anything but the most critical of functions. Let us further assume that the sheriff of this town knows who has committed the murders and that the murderer has died in his sleep. But the sheriff cannot prove to the town that this individual is guilty (the townspeople would just assume that the sheriff is making up the story in order to shirk his duties). However, there is a drifter passing through town that the sheriff knows can be framed for the murders. Our sheriff performs the utilitarian calculations and determines that the gain in a feeling of security for the town outweighs the harm of going to jail for this one individual, and so frames him for the killings.

Here the individual is subjected to a great harm in order to produce a proportionally lesser benefit to others. I take it that no one would consider the act morally acceptable. This illuminates the widespread moral intuition that causing a great harm for a lesser benefit, even to a great number of people, cannot be morally justified. Most people would even consider it wrong to incur a great harm to a few in order to produce a great benefit to the many, such as removing the eyes from a sighted man and implanting them in two blind persons so that they can now see (with only a drop off in peripheral vision and depth perception distinguishing them from those with two eyes). There are even some who believe that no amount of harm to an individual can be justified on grounds that it will benefit others, since harms and benefits are incommensurable commodities. Given that statistics demonstrate that downsizing often leads to the loss of home and even suicide, it seems hard to deny that at least some downsized workers incur a significant harm from the practice. On the other side, since investors in a large corporation tend to diversify their assets, they incur only a minor benefit when any one stock price rises. Thus, if the act of downsizing is not done as a means of saving the corporation—preventing more workers from losing their jobs—but rather to increase profits, it involves causing a great harm for a minor benefit.

We can also draw a distinction within the practice of downsizing which will serve to amplify its wrongfulness in certain circumstances. Ask yourself if there is a difference in the moral status of the following two acts: First, a country involved in a just war bombs the other side's munitions factory in order to end the war, knowing that the bombing will also destroy a grade school bordering the factory and thus killing ten children. Second, a country in a just war bombs the school where the leaders of the opposing country send their kids in order to get them to end the war (accidentally destroying the neighboring munitions factory in the process). Most people would agree that the latter act is far worse than the former. The best way to explain this intuition is that in the latter act, the death of the children is a means to ending the war, while in the former it is an unfortunate byproduct of that means. The children in the second act are being *used* in a way that they are not being used in the former act.

Now consider the case where a CEO downsizes under the knowledge that the mere news of these layoffs will be greeted favorably by the stock market, and thus cause stock prices to rise . . . as opposed to the case where downsizing will improve profits by increasing productivity. Here the very act that harms the workers—the loss of their jobs—itself produces the benefit to shareholders. Harm is not a simple byproduct of an act which independently brings benefit, but rather is the means to that benefit. This grates even more deeply against our intuitions that it is wrong to use individuals for others' benefit.

Legitimate Expectations

We might also approach the issue from the perspective of the legitimate expectations of the individuals involved. To illustrate this notion, consider the possibility that the federal government repeals the home interest tax break without any other modifications in the tax code. While I see no reason why homeowners, and not renters, deserve such a break, one could question the action on grounds that homeowners have made plans under the assumption that this break would continue. Those who lose their homes because of the change in the tax laws would have a legitimate complaint, even though there was never a written guarantee that current tax laws would remain forever unchanged. Similarly, workers have made plans under the assumption of a continued source of income. These are not simply plans for leisure activities such as vacations, but rather plans that impinge upon their fundamental well-being as well as the well-being of their families. There are, however, no similar expectations on the part of the shareholder. For one, shareholders know that stock prices are volatile and that they take a risk when entering the market. Thus, no reasonable investor backs her home on the future performance of her securities. Investors may expect a certain average rate of return, but this is over the long term and they budget accordingly. They do not bank important items such as their homes on the assumption of the continued unprecedented rates of return seen in the past few years. Surely, these returns are treated as "icing on the cake," and thus if preserving jobs will diminish returns to the levels historically expected from the market, no critical expectations are thwarted. Also, as mentioned earlier, shareholders tend to consider the companies in which they invest to have obligations to parties other than themselves. Hence, one cannot plead that shareholders entered the market expecting that the company would be run solely for their own benefit.

Fairness

We may also appeal to the work of John Rawls to provide critical perspective on the issue.[16] . . . I will draw upon what I consider his more central intuition: that the arbitrary conditions of one's situation ought not to count against one's life prospects. The idea here is that the individual does not deserve the rewards or punishments that come via things for which she is not responsible. At the very least, these factors include genetic endowments and the social institutions of the society in which she lives.

This seems to me a very strong intuition, one that can account for a wide variety of common moral responses. Consider, for instance, the indignation fans often feel toward professional athletes who receive an exorbitant degree of compensation for their efforts. Physical talents have a considerable genetic component, meaning that much of a top athlete's skill is due to choosing his parents more wisely than the average person. Moreover, these people were lucky enough to be born in a society that happens to value their particular skills, also not something for which they can claim credit. While they might have worked hard to develop their natural talents, there is no reason to think that they have put in more effort than the less talented; and any differences in effort are certainly not great enough to merit the incredible differences in compensation.

To apply the principle here, we would first note that the worker who loses his job does so through no fault of his own. Someone fired due to incompetence is not downsized. Downsizing does not involve a surgical removal of all employees in a firm whose work is not up to snuff; instead, whole divisions are removed by virtue of their overall profitability, with no effort made to determine if individual members of those divisions are at fault. In fact, if a division or plant is unprofitable it is most likely due to mismanagement on the part of those running the corporation. This is perhaps one of the reasons why downsized workers feel betrayed, as no attempt is made by management to judge their actual job performance. Downsized workers find themselves harmed due to forces outside of their control. Moreover, these forces have conspired to selectively harm them since upper management tends to be insulated from these harms, by devices such as receiving a sizable "golden parachute" when dismissed. True, there are a variety of ways in which natural and social forces reward and punish arbitrarily but this does not make those harms permissible or release us from obligations to mitigate them.

On the other side, shareholders have done nothing to merit the sharp gains that downsizing produces. Perhaps they are owed good faith efforts at sound management by the corporation in virtue of their investment, but they cannot claim to deserve the special increases in the value of their investments due solely to laying off workers. The fact that we happen to live in a world where canning large numbers of workers is a quick means of increasing profits is not any of their doing. Note also that those shareholders who have invested through mutual funds have not themselves chosen to invest in this particular firm. These investors most likely have little idea as to which stocks their mutual funds actually hold, since one of the appeals of these funds is that they allow individuals to enter the market without the need to concern themselves with the intricacies of investing, or the day-to-day fluctuations of the market. . . .

IV. APPLYING THE RESULTS AND RELATED CONCERNS

. . . Business managers will need to examine the actual situations of their shareholders and workers, as well as that of the company, in order to ascertain if a decision to downsize is morally permissible. While this grants that some acts of downsizing may be morally permissible, simply establishing that corporate managers cannot lay claim to a special duty to shareholders that trumps any competing duties cuts against the grain of much of corporate America's current philosophy. For instance, in a speech to business representatives, David Rockefeller argued that corporations "have a responsibility to society beyond that of maximizing profits for shareholders." Yet he quickly qualified this position by stating that "let me add, before they come to retract my Chicago degree, that making profits must come first." While many business persons would agree that corporations have some obligations to persons besides shareholders, all but the most socially conscious would likely consider anathema the position that these obligations stand on equal footing with obligations to shareholders. . . .

How might the corporate manager apply the insights gathered here to a particular situation? First and foremost, an act of downsizing that prevents the collapse of the corporation can be justified on grounds that the organism is saved by amputating a limb. However, we must keep in mind that bankruptcy does not always mean the complete shutting down of shop. Bankruptcy courts make every effort to find a way of restructuring the debts of the corporation to keep it in business. In fact, corporations have been known to use bankruptcy as a means of avoiding a court settlement. But an act of downsizing that merely increases profits which seems increasingly the case, requires a careful analysis of the harms and benefits it will incur to the parties involved. For a small firm, such as a fast-food franchise with a single proprietor, the owner may be at greater risk than her employees. The owner most likely has a large percentage of her personal fortune wrapped up in the company, whereas the workers are usually (but not always) high school students just earning extra spending money. However, with a large corporation, the results are likely to be quite different. It bears mention that the corporate entity is grounded in the principle that a separation exists between the corporation and the personal finances of its owners, a device created specifically to minimize the risk to shareholders. Thus, the owner of a corporation is not personally liable for its debts; if IBM dissolves, shareholders need not fear that IBM's creditors will come knocking at their doors. Legal protection to the shareholder is built into the corporation's charter. More importantly, since investors tend not to risk money that is required for their sustenance, their losses do not normally affect their immediate well-being. By contrast, the worker who banks his home on his job places his immediate well-being, as well as the well-being of his family, in far greater peril. Finally, investors today diversify their assets through mutual funds which own shares in thousands of corporations. Thus, losses from one stock create only a minor shift in the fund's overall value. This means that acts of downsizing can cause great harm to a few for a minor benefit to the many, something that I have argued is not morally permissible. Also, one can argue that the sole proprietor who has nursed the business from the ground up merits greater consideration than the mutual fund investor who may not even know that he or she owns shares in the corporation. Moreover, the worker who has purchased a home, and started a family, based on the assumption of the continued source of income, is deserving of greater consideration than the investor who finds that unprecedented gains in the stock market allow him to extend his vacation to Aruba by a week. . . .

Why has the philosophical community ignored the issue of corporate downsizing? Perhaps this is due to the perception that challenges to the practice would strike at the heart of the free market system, and thus would likely emanate from a Marxist, or other similarly passé philosophical systems. But I hope to have demonstrated that the issue can be tackled with garden-variety moral intuitions, ones that appeal to nothing more exotic than principles pertaining to the fundamental moral equality of humans. These arguments may provoke objections, but they are intended to initiate discussion on a topic long in need of careful examination.

NOTES

1. Richard L. Bunning, "The Dynamics of Downsizing," *Personnel Journal* 69, no. 9 (Sept. 1990): 69.
2. Interview with Secretary of Labor Robert Reich in *Challenge*, July/August

1996, 4. Reich notes that while the *average* wage is up, the *median* wage (the wage of the individual in the middle) is down. The discrepancy is due to the unprecedented rise in compensation for top executives during the 1980s and 1990s.

3. Downsizing by the auto industry in the 1970s and 1980s caused Flint, Michigan's unemployment rate to climb to the highest in the United States, and its crime rate to rise accordingly. *Facts About the Cities,* ed. Allan Carpenter (New York: H. W. Wilson Co., 1992).

4. Harvey M. Brenner, *Mental Illness and the Economy* (Cambridge: Harvard University Press, 1973); Ralph Catalano and David Dooley, "Economic Predictors of Depressed Mood and Stressful Life Events in a Metropolitan Community," *Journal of Health and Social Behavior* 18 (1977): 292–307; Jean Hartley, Dan Jacobson, Bert Klandermans, and Tinka van Vuuren, *Job Insecurity: Coping With Jobs at Risk* (Newbury Park: Sage, 1991); and John R. Reynolds, "The Effects of Industrial Employment Conditions on Job-Related Distress," *Journal of Health and Social Behavior* (June 1997): 105–18.

5. David Dooley, Ralph Catalano, and Karen S. Rook, "Personal and Aggregate Unemployment and Psychological Symptoms," *Journal of Social Issues* 44 (1988): 107–23; David Dooley, Ralph Catalano, and Georjeanna Wilson, "Depression and Unemployment: Panel Findings from the Epidemiologic Catchment Area Study," *American Journal of Community Health* 22 (1994): 745–65.

6. Ian Maitland, "The Morality of the Corporation: An Empirical or Normative Disagreement?" *Business Ethics Quarterly* 4, no. 4 (1994): 445–57.

7. Maitland, op. cit., 449.

8. Maitland, op. cit., 450.

9. Larry D. Sonderquist and Robert P. Vecchio, "Reconciling Shareholders' Rights and Corporate Responsibility: New Guidelines for Management," *Duke Law Journal* (1978): 840; reproduced in John R. Boatright, "Fiduciary Duties and the Shareholder-Management Relation: Or, What's So Special About Shareholders?" *Business Ethics Quarterly* 4, no. 4 (October 1994): 398.

10. Boatright, op. cit., 397.

11. Reich, op. cit.

12. Maitland, op. cit., 451.

13. Friedman, "The Social Responsibility of Business Is to Increase Its Profits," *New York Times Magazine,* September 1970, reprinted in *Ethical Theory and Business,* ed. Tom L. Beauchamp and Norman E. Bowie (Englewood Cliffs, NJ: Prentice Hall, 1979), 136–38.

14. Wayne F. Cascio, interview on National Public Radio, November 14, 1997.

15. Reich, op. cit.

16. John Rawls, *A Theory of Justice* (Cambridge: Cambridge University Press, 1971).

REVIEW AND DISCUSSION QUESTIONS

1. Orlando distinguishes property for private use and property for profit, using the example of a landlord renting an apartment. Do you find the example persuasive? Explain why or why not.
2. Critically assess each of the six arguments supporting the proposition that shareholders take priority over workers and Orlando's responses to each. Which of the arguments are the strongest? Which do you see as the weakest? Do you agree that there is moral equality between workers and shareholders? If so, what implications does this have?
3. Can downsizing be supported on utilitarian grounds? Explain why or why not.
4. Is downsizing wrong because it is an instance of "harming some to benefit others," as Orlando argues?
5. Orlando's "legitimate expectations" argument against downsizing rests on the premise that "workers have made plans under the assumption of a continued source of income." Is that premise true and, if so, was it reasonable for workers to make this assumption?
6. Orlando appeals to the example of highly paid professional athletes to support the principle that people do not deserve rewards or punishments for things for which they are not responsible. Do you find that example persuasive? Do you accept Orlando's principle? If so, does it show that downsizing is wrong?
7. Assess the contention that Orlando's critique of downsizing ends up challenging the free market system itself.

SUGGESTIONS FOR FURTHER READING

For a good discussion of the human costs of downsizing, see the *New York Times* report, *The Downsizing of America* (Random House 1996). For the debate over shareholder interests, see David E. Shrader, "The Oddness of Corporate Ownership," *Journal of Social Philosophy* 27 (Fall 1996), John R. Boatright, "Fiduciary Duties and the Shareholder Management Relationship: Or, What's So Special About Shareholders?" *Business Ethics Quarterly* 4 (October 1994), and the essays by Friedman, Carson, and Goodpaster, cited in the Suggestions for Further Reading at the end of the previous essay. On the related topic of plant shutdowns and relocations, see John P. Kavanagh, "Ethical Issues in Plant Relocation," in William H. Shaw and Vincent Barry, *Moral Issues in Business*, 8th ed. (Wadsworth 2001), and Judith Lichtenberg, "On Alternatives to Industrial Flight: The Moral Issues," *Report from the Institute for Philosophy and Public Policy* 4 (Fall 1984).

◆

CHAPTER FOUR

The Great Non-Debate Over International Sweatshops

Ian Maitland

These days, contractors in third world countries such as Indonesia and China manufacture most of the shoes, shirts, and other clothing that large American footwear and apparel companies such as Nike and Levi Strauss sell. Critics have lambasted this practice because of the exceedingly low wages and poor working conditions that frequently characterize these "sweatshops." In this provocative essay, however, Ian Maitland, a management professor at the University of Minnesota, defends international sweatshops against the charge of exploitation on both factual and ethical grounds. He examines and rejects the idea that sweatshops pay unconscionable wages, that they impoverish local workers and widen the gap between rich and poor, and that American companies collude with repressive regimes that stifle dissent and repress workers. Arguing that interfering with the market can have terrible results, he concludes not only that paying market wages in developing countries is morally permissible, but also that it may be morally wrong for companies to pay wages that exceed market levels.

THINGS TO CONSIDER

1. Maitland believes that the controversy over international sweatshops is really a "non-debate." Explain why.
2. What are the four possible standards that have been proposed for setting wages and labor standards in international sweatshops?
3. What are the four main charges or arguments that make up the case against international sweatshops?
4. Maitland believes that attempting to improve upon market wages and working conditions can have dire results. Explain his reasoning.

Reprinted by permission from the *British Academy of Management Annual Conference Proceedings*, September 1997.

In recent years, there has been a dramatic growth in the contracting out of production by companies in the industrialized countries to suppliers in developing countries. This globalization of production has led to an emerging international division of labor in footwear and apparel in which companies like Nike and Reebok concentrate on product design and marketing but rely on a network of contractors in Indonesia, China, Central America, etc., to build shoes or sew shirts according to exact specifications and deliver a high quality good according to precise delivery schedules. As Nike's vice president for Asia has put it, "We don't know the first thing about manufacturing. We are marketers and designers."

The contracting arrangements have drawn intense fire from critics— usually labor and human rights activists. The "critics" (as I will refer to them) have charged that the companies are (by proxy) exploiting workers in the plants (which I will call "international sweatshops") of their suppliers. Specifically, the companies stand accused of chasing cheap labor around the globe, failing to pay their workers living wages, using child labor, turning a blind eye to abuses of human rights, and being complicit with repressive regimes in denying workers the right to join unions and failing to enforce minimum labor standards in the workplace, and so on.

The campaign against international sweatshops has largely unfolded on television and, to a lesser extent, in the print media. What seems like no more than a handful of critics has mounted an aggressive, media-savvy campaign that has put the publicity-shy retail giants on the defensive. The critics have orchestrated a series of sensational "disclosures" on prime time television exposing the terrible pay and working conditions in factories making jeans for Levi's or sneakers for Nike or Pocahontas shirts for Disney. One of the principal scourge of the companies has been Charles Kernaghan who runs the National Labor Coalition (NLC), a labor human rights group involving twenty-five unions. It was Kernaghan who . . . broke the news before a Congressional committee that Kathie Lee Gifford's clothing line was being made by thirteen- and fourteen-years-olds working twenty hour days in factories in Honduras. Kernaghan also arranged for teenage workers from sweatshops in Central America to testify before congressional committees about abusive labor practices. At one of these hearings, one of the workers held up a Liz Claiborne cotton sweater identical to ones she had sewn since she was a thirteen-year-old working twelve hour days. . . . According to a news report, "[t]his image, accusations of oppressive conditions at the factory and the Claiborne logo played well on that evening's network news."[1] The result has been a circus-like atmosphere—as in Roman circus where Christians were thrown to lions.

Kernaghan has shrewdly targeted the companies' carefully cultivated public images. He has explained: "Their image is everything. They live and die by their image. That gives you a certain power over them." As a result, he says, "these companies are sitting ducks. They have no leg to stand on. That's why it's possible for a tiny group like us to take on a giant like Wal-Mart. You can't defend paying someone 31 cents an hour in Honduras. . . ."[2] Apparently most of the companies agree with Kernaghan. Not a single company has tried to mount a serious defense of its contracting practices. They have judged that they cannot win a war of soundbites with the critics. Instead of making a fight of it, the companies have sued for peace in order to protect their principal asset—their image.

Major U.S. retailers have responded by adopting codes of conduct on human and labor rights in their international operations. Levi Strauss, Nike, Sears, JCPenney, Wal-Mart, Home Depot, Philips Van-Heusen now have such codes. . . . Peter Jacobi, President of Global Sourcing for Levi Strauss has advised: "If your company owns a popular brand, protect this priceless asset at all costs. Highly visible companies have any number of reasons to conduct their business not just responsibly but also in ways that cannot be portrayed as unfair, illegal, or unethical. This sets an extremely high standard since it must be applied to both company-owned businesses and contractors. . . ."[3] And according to another Levi Strauss spokesman, "In many respects, we're protecting our single largest asset: our brand image and corporate reputation." . . .

Recently a truce of sorts between the critics and the companies was announced. . . . A presidential task force, including representatives of labor unions, human rights groups, and apparel companies such as L.L. Bean and Nike, has come up with a set of voluntary standards which, it hopes, will be embraced by the entire industry. Companies that comply with the code will be entitled to use a "No Sweat" label.

OBJECTIVE OF THIS PAPER

In this confrontation between the companies and their critics, neither side seems to have judged it to be in its interest to seriously engage the issue at the heart of this controversy, namely: What are appropriate wages and labor standards in international sweatshops? As we have seen, the companies have treated the charges about sweatshops as a public relations problem to be managed so as to minimize harm to their public images. The critics have apparently judged that the best way to keep public indignation at boiling point is to oversimplify the issue and treat it as a morality play featuring heartless exploiters and victimized third world workers. The result has been a great non-debate over international sweatshops. Paradoxically, if peace breaks out between the two sides, the chances that the debate will be seriously joined may recede still further. Indeed, there exists a real risk (I will argue) that any such truce may be a collusive one that will come at the expense of the very third world workers it is supposed to help.

This paper takes up the issue of what are appropriate wages and labor standards in international sweatshops. Critics charge that the present arrangements are exploitative. I proceed by examining the specific charges of exploitation from the standpoints of both (a) their factual and (b) their ethical sufficiency. . . .

WHAT ARE ETHICALLY APPROPRIATE LABOR STANDARDS IN INTERNATIONAL SWEATSHOPS?

What are ethically acceptable or appropriate levels of wages and labor standards in international sweatshops? The following four possibilities just about run the gamut of standards or principles that have been seriously proposed to regulate such policies.

1. *Home-country standards:* It might be argued (and in rare cases has been) that international corporations have an ethical duty to pay the same wages and provide the same labor standards regardless of where they operate. However, the view that home-country standards should apply in host countries is rejected by most business ethicists and (officially at least) by the critics of international sweatshops. Thus, Thomas Donaldson argues that "[b]y arbitrarily establishing U.S. wage levels as the bench mark for fairness one eliminates the

role of the international market in establishing salary levels, and this in turn eliminates the incentive U.S. corporations have to hire foreign workers."[4] Richard De George makes much the same argument: If there were a rule that said "that American MNCs [multinational corporations] that wish to be ethical must pay the same wages abroad as they do at home. . . . [then] MNCs would have little incentive to move their manufacturing abroad; and if they did move abroad they would disrupt the local labor market with artificially high wages that bore no relation to the local standard or cost of living."[5]

2. *"Living wage" standard:* It has been proposed that an international corporation should, at a minimum, pay a "living wage." Thus, De George says that corporations should pay a living wage "even when this is not paid by local firms."[6] However, it is hard to pin down what this means operationally. According to De George, a living wage should "allow the worker to live in dignity as a human being." In order to respect the human rights of its workers, he says, a corporation must pay "at least subsistence wages and as much above that as workers and their dependents need to live with reasonable dignity, given the general state of development of the society." As we shall see, the living wage standard has become a rallying cry of the critics of international sweatshops. Apparently, De George believes that it is preferable for a corporation to provide no job at all than to offer one that pays less than a living wage.

3. *Donaldson's test:* Thomas Donaldson believes that "it is irrelevant whether the standards of the host country comply or fail to comply with home country standards; what is relevant is whether they meet a universal, objective minimum." He tries to specify "a moral minimum for the behavior of all international economic agents."[7] However, he concedes . . . that "many rights . . . are dependent for their specification on the level of economic development of the country in question."[8] Accordingly, he proposes a test to determine when deviations from home-country standards are unethical. That test provides as follows: "The practice is permissible if and only if the members of the home country would, under conditions of economic development relevantly similar to those of the host country, regard the practice as permissible."[9] Donaldson's test is vulnerable to Bernard Shaw's objection to the Golden Rule, namely that we should not do unto others as we would they do unto us, because their tastes may be different. The test also complicates matters by introducing

counterfactuals and hypotheticals (if I were in their place [which I'm not] what would I want?). This indeterminacy is a serious weakness in an ethical code: It is likely to confuse managers who want to act ethically and to provide loopholes for those don't.

4. *Classical liberal standard:* Finally, there is what I will call the classical liberal standard. According to this standard a practice (wage or labor practice) is ethically acceptable if it is freely chosen by informed workers. For example, in a recent report the World Bank invoked this standard in connection with workplace safety. It said: "The appropriate level is therefore that at which the costs are commensurate with the value that informed workers place on improved working conditions and reduced risk."[10] Most business ethicists reject this standard on the grounds that there is some sort of market failure or the "background conditions" are lacking for markets to work effectively. Thus, for Donaldson full (or near-full) employment is a prerequisite if workers are to make sound choices regarding workplace safety: "The average level of unemployment in the developing countries today exceeds 40 percent, a figure that has frustrated the application of neoclassical economic principles to the international economy on a score of issues. With full employment, and all other things being equal, market forces will encourage workers to make trade-offs between job opportunities using safety as a variable. But with massive unemployment, market forces in developing countries drive the unemployed to the jobs they are lucky enough to land, regardless of the safety."[11] . . . De George, too, believes that the necessary conditions are lacking for market forces to operate benignly. Without what he calls "background institutions" to protect the workers and the resources of the developing country (e.g., enforceable minimum wages) and/or greater equality of bargaining power exploitation is the most likely result.[12] . . .

THE CASE AGAINST INTERNATIONAL SWEATSHOPS

To many of their critics, international sweatshops exemplify the way in which the greater openness of the world economy is hurting workers. According to one critic, "as it is now constituted, the world trading system discriminates against workers, especially those in the Third World."[13] Globalization means a transition from (more or less) regulated domestic economies to an unregulated world economy.

The superior mobility of capital, and the essentially fixed, immobile nature of world labor, means a fundamental shift in bargaining power in favor of large international corporations. Their global reach permits them to shift production almost costlessly from one location to another. As a consequence, instead of being able to exercise some degree of control over companies operating within their borders, governments are now locked in a bidding war with one another to attract and retain the business of large multinational companies.

The critics allege that international companies are using the threat of withdrawal or withholding of investment to pressure governments and workers to grant concessions. "Today [multinational companies] choose between workers in developing countries that compete against each other to depress wages to attract foreign investment."[14] The result is a race for the bottom—a "destructive downward bidding spiral of the labor conditions and wages of workers throughout the world. . . ." Thus, critics charge that in Indonesia wages are deliberately held below the poverty level or subsistence in order to make the country a desirable location. The results of this competitive dismantling of worker protections, living standards and worker rights are predictable: deteriorating work conditions, declining real incomes for workers, and a widening gap between rich and poor in developing countries. I turn next to the specific charges made by the critics of international sweatshops.

Unconscionable Wages

Critics charge that the companies, by their proxies, are paying "starvation wages" and "slave wages." They are far from clear about what wage level they consider to be appropriate. But they generally demand that companies pay a "living wage." . . . According to Tim Smith, wage levels should be "fair, decent or a living wage for an employee and his or her family." He has said that wages in the maquiladoras of Mexico averaged $35 to $55 a week (in or near 1993) which he calls a "shockingly substandard wage," apparently on the grounds that it "clearly does not allow an employee to feed and care for a family adequately."[15] In 1992, Nike came in for harsh criticism when a magazine published the pay stub of a worker at one of its Indonesian suppliers. It showed that the worker was paid at the rate of $1.03 per day which was reportedly less than the Indonesian government's figure for "minimum physical need."[16]

Immiserization Thesis

Former Labor Secretary Robert Reich has proposed as a test of the fairness of development policies that "[l]ow-wage workers should become better off, not worse off, as trade and investment boost national income." He has written that "[i]f a country pursues policies that . . . limit to a narrow elite the benefits of trade, the promise of open commerce is perverted and drained of its rationale."[17] A key claim of the activists is that companies actually impoverish or immiserize developing country workers. They experience an absolute decline in living standards. This thesis follows from the claim that the bidding war among developing countries is depressing wages. . . .

Widening Gap Between Rich and Poor

A related charge is that international sweatshops are contributing to the increasing gap between rich and poor. Not only are the poor being absolutely impoverished, but trade is generating greater inequality within developing countries. Another test that Reich has proposed to establish the fairness of international trade is that "the gap between rich and poor should tend to narrow with development, not widen."[18] Critics charge that international sweatshops flunk that test. They say that the increasing GNPs of some developing countries simply mask a widening gap between rich and poor. "Across the world, both local and foreign elites are getting richer from the exploitation of the most vulnerable."[19] And, "The major adverse consequence of quickening global economic integration has been widening income disparity within almost all nations. . . ."[20] There appears to be a tacit alliance between the elites of both first and third worlds to exploit the most vulnerable, to regiment and control and conscript them so that they can create the material conditions for the elites' extravagant lifestyles.

Collusion with Repressive Regimes

Critics charge that, in their zeal to make their countries safe for foreign investment, third world regimes, notably China and Indonesia, have stepped up their repression. Not only have these countries failed to enforce even the minimal labor rules on the books, but they have also used their military and police to break strikes and repress independent unions. They have stifled political dissent, both to retain their hold on political power and to avoid any instability that might scare off foreign investors. Consequently, critics charge, companies such as Nike are profiting from political repression. "As unions spread in [Korea and Taiwan], Nike shifted its suppliers primarily to Indonesia, China and Thailand, where they could depend on governments to suppress independent union-organizing efforts."[21]

EVALUATION OF THE CHARGES AGAINST INTERNATIONAL SWEATSHOPS

The critics' charges are undoubtedly accurate on a number of points: (1) There is no doubt that international companies are chasing cheap labor. (2) The wages paid by the international sweatshops are—by American standards—shockingly low. (3) Some developing country governments have tightly controlled or repressed organized labor in order to prevent it from disturbing the flow of foreign investment. Thus, in Indonesia, independent unions have been suppressed. (4) It is not unusual in developing countries for minimum wage levels to be lower than the official poverty level. (5) Developing country governments have winked at violations of minimum wage laws and labor rules. However, most jobs are in the informal sector and so largely, outside the scope of government supervision. (6) Some suppliers have employed children or have subcontracted work to other producers who have done so. (7) Some developing country governments deny their people basic political rights. China is the obvious example; Indonesia's record is pretty horrible but had shown steady improvement until the last two years. But on many of the other counts, the critics' charges appear to be seriously inaccurate. And, even where the charges are accurate, it is not self-evident that the practices in question are improper or unethical, as we see next.

Wages and Conditions

Even the critics of international sweatshops do not dispute that the wages they pay are generally higher than—or at least equal to—comparable wages in the labor markets where they operate. According to the International Labor Organization (ILO), multinational companies often apply standards relating to wages, benefits, conditions of work, and occupational safety and health that both exceed statutory requirements and those practised by local firms. The ILO also says that wages and working conditions in so-called Export Processing Zones (EPZs) are often equal to or higher than jobs outside.[22] The World Bank says that the poorest workers in developing countries work in the informal sector where they often earn less than half what a formal sector employee earns. Moreover, "informal and rural workers often must work under more hazardous and insecure conditions than their formal sector counterparts."[23]

The same appears to hold true for the international sweatshops. In 1996, young women working in the plant of a Nike supplier in Serang, Indonesia were earning the Indonesian legal minimum wage of 5,200 rupiahs or about $2.28 each day. As a report in the *Washington Post* pointed out, just earning the minimum wage put these workers among higher-paid Indonesians: "In Indonesia, less than half the working population earns the minimum wage, since about half of all adults here are in farming, and the typical farmer would make only about 2,000 rupiahs each day."[24] . . . Also in 1996, a Nike spokeswoman estimated that an entry-level factory worker in the plant of a Nike supplier made five times what a farmer makes. Nike's chairman, Phil Knight, likes to teasingly remind critics that the average worker in one of Nike's Chinese factories is paid more than a professor at Beijing University. There is also plentiful anecdotal evidence from non-Nike sources. A worker at the Taiwanese-owned King Star Garment Assembly plant in Honduras told a reporter that he was earning seven times what he earned in the countryside.[25] In Bangladesh, the country's fledgling garment industry was paying women who had never worked before between $40 and $55 a month in 1991. That compared with a national per capita income of about $200 and the approximately $1 a day earned by many of these women's husbands as day laborers or rickshaw drivers.[26] . . .

There is also the mute testimony of the lines of job applicants outside the sweatshops in Guatemala and Honduras. According to Lucy Martinez-Mont, in Guatemala the sweatshops are conspicuous for the long lines of young people waiting to be interviewed for a job.[27] Outside the gates of an industrial park in Honduras . . . "anxious onlookers are always waiting, hoping for a chance at least to fill out a job application [for employment at one of the apparel plants]."[28]

The critics of sweatshops acknowledge that workers have voluntarily taken their jobs, consider themselves lucky to have them, and want to keep them. . . . But they go on to discount the workers' views as the product of confusion or ignorance, and/or they just argue that the workers' views are beside the point. Thus, while "it is undoubtedly true" that Nike has given jobs to thousands of people who wouldn't be working otherwise, they say that "neatly skirts the fundamental human-rights issue raised by these production arrangements that are now spreading all across the world."[29] Similarly, the NLC's Kernaghan says that "[w]hether workers think they are better off in the assembly plants than elsewhere is not the real issue." Kernaghan, and Jeff Ballinger of the AFL-CIO, concede that the workers desperately need these jobs. But "[t]hey say they're not asking that U.S. companies stop operating in these countries. They're asking that workers be paid a living wage and treated like human beings."[30] Apparently these workers are victims of what Marx called false consciousness, or else they would grasp that they are being exploited. According to Barnet and Cavanagh, "For many workers . . . exploitation is not a concept easily comprehended because the alternative prospects for earning a living are so bleak."[31]

Immiserization and Inequality

The critics' claim that the countries that host international sweatshops are marked by growing poverty and inequality is flatly contradicted by the record. In fact, many of those countries have experienced sharp increases in living standards—for all strata of society. In trying to attract investment in simple manufacturing, Malaysia and Indonesia and, now, Vietnam and China are retracing the industrialization path already successfully taken by East Asian countries such as Taiwan, Korea, Singapore, and Hong Kong. These four countries got their start by producing labor-intensive manufactured goods (often electrical and electronic components, shoes, and garments) for export markets. Over time they graduated to the export of higher value-added items that are skill-intensive and require a relatively developed industrial base.

As is well known, these East Asian countries achieved growth rates have been exceeding eight percent for a quarter-century. . . . The workers in these economies were not impoverished by growth. The benefits of growth were widely diffused: These economies achieved essentially full employment in the 1960s. Real wages rose by as much as a factor of four. Absolute poverty fell. And income inequality remained at low to moderate levels. It is true that in the initial stages the rapid growth generated only moderate increases in wages. But once essentially full employment was reached, . . . the increased demand for labor resulted in the bidding up of wages as firms competed for a scarce labor supply.

Interestingly, given its historic mission as a watchdog for international labor standards, the ILO has embraced this development model. It recently noted that the most successful developing economies, in terms of output and employment growth, have been "those who best exploited emerging opportunities in the global economy."[32] An "export-oriented policy is vital in countries that are starting on the industrialization path and have large surpluses of cheap labour." Countries that have succeeded in attracting foreign direct investment (FDI) have experienced rapid growth in manufacturing output and exports. The successful attraction of foreign investment in plant and equipment "can be a powerful spur to rapid industrialization and employment creation." . . .

According to the World Bank, the rapidly growing Asian economies (including Indonesia) "have also been unusually successful at sharing the fruits of their growth."[33] In fact, while inequality in the West has been growing, it has been shrinking in the Asian economies. They are the only economies in the world to have experienced high growth *and* declining inequality, and they also show shrinking gender gaps in education. . . .

Profiting from Repression?

What about the charge that international sweatshops are profiting from repression? It is undeniable that there is repression in many of the countries where sweatshops are located. But economic development appears to be relaxing that repression rather than strengthening its grip. The companies are supposed to benefit from government policies (e.g., repression of unions) that hold down labor costs. However, as we have seen, the wages paid by the international sweatshops already match or exceed the prevailing local wages. Not only that, but incomes in the East Asian economies, and in Indonesia, have risen rapidly. Moreover, even the sweatshops' critics admit that the main factor restraining wages in countries like Indonesia is the state of the labor market. . . . The high rate of unemployment and underemployment acts as a brake on wages: Only about 55 percent of the Indonesian labor force can find more than thirty-five hours of work each week, and about two million workers are unemployed.

The critics, however, are right in saying that the Indonesian government has opposed independent unions in the sweatshops out of fear they would lead to higher wages and labor unrest. But the government's fear clearly is that unions might drive wages in the modern industrial sector *above* market-clearing levels—or, more exactly, farther above market. . . . I think we can safely take at face value its claims that its policies are genuinely intended to help the economy create jobs to absorb the massive numbers of unemployed and underemployed.

LABOR STANDARDS IN INTERNATIONAL SWEATSHOPS: PAINFUL TRADE-OFFS

Who but the grinch could grudge paying a few additional pennies to some of the world's poorest workers? There is no doubt that the rhetorical force of the critics' case against international sweatshops rests on this apparently self-evident proposition. However, higher wages and improved labor standards are not free. After all, the critics themselves attack companies for chasing cheap labor. It follows that, if labor in developing countries is made more expensive (say, as the result of pressure by the critics), then those countries will receive less foreign investment, and fewer jobs will be created there. Imposing higher wages may deprive these countries of the one comparative advantage they enjoy, namely low-cost labor. . . .

By itself that may or may not be ethically objectionable. But these higher wages come at the expense of the incomes and the job opportunities of much poorer workers. As economists explain, higher wages in the formal sector reduce employment there and (by increasing the supply of labor) depress incomes in the informal sector. The case against requiring above-market wages for international sweatshop workers is essentially the same as the case against other measures that artificially raise labor costs, such as the minimum wage. In Jagdish Bhagwati's words: "Requiring a minimum wage in an overpopulated, developing country, as is done in a developed country, may actually be morally wicked. A minimum wage might help the unionized, industrial proletariat, while limiting the ability to save and invest rapidly which is necessary to draw more of the unemployed and nonunionized rural poor into gainful employment and income."[34] The World Bank makes the same point: "Minimum wages may help the most poverty-stricken workers in industrial countries, but they clearly do not in developing nations. . . . The workers whom minimum wage legislation tries to protect—urban formal workers—already earn much more than the less favored majority. . . . And inasmuch as minimum wage and other regulations discourage formal employment by increasing wage and nonwage costs, they hurt the poor who aspire to formal employment."[35]

The story is no different when it comes to labor standards other than wages. If standards are set too high they will hurt investment and employment. The World Bank report points out that "[r]educing hazards in the workplace is costly, and typically the greater the reduction the more it costs. Moreover, the costs of compliance often fall largely on employees through lower wages or reduced employment. As a result, setting standards too high can actually lower workers' welfare. . . ." Perversely, if the higher standards advocated by critics retard the growth of formal sector jobs, then that will trap more informal and rural workers in jobs that are far more hazardous and insecure than those of their formal sector counterparts. . . .

Of course it might be objected that trading off workers' rights for more jobs is unethical. But, so far as I can determine, the critics have not made this argument. Although they sometimes implicitly accept the existence of the trade-off (we saw that they attack Nike for chasing cheap labor), their public statements are silent on the lost or forgone jobs from higher wages and better labor standards. At other times, they imply or claim that improvements in workers' wages and conditions are essentially free: According to Kernaghan, "Companies could easily double their employees' wages, and it would be nothing."

In summary, the result of the ostensibly humanitarian changes urged by critics are likely to be (1) reduced employment in the formal or modern sector of the economy, (2) lower incomes in the informal sector, (3) less investment and so slower economic growth, (4) reduced exports, (5) greater inequality and poverty. . . .

CONCLUSION: THE CASE FOR NOT EXCEEDING MARKET STANDARDS

It is part of the job description of business ethicists to exhort companies to treat their workers better (otherwise what purpose do they serve?). So it will have come as no surprise that both the business ethicists whose views I summarized at the beginning of this paper– Thomas Donaldson and Richard De George–objected to letting the market alone determine wages and labor standards in multinational companies. Both of them proposed criteria for setting wages that might occasionally "improve" on the outcomes of the market.

Their reasons for rejecting market determination of wages were similar. They both cited conditions that allegedly prevent international markets from generating ethically acceptable results. Donaldson argued that neoclassical economic principles are not applicable to international business because of high unemployment rates in developing countries. And De George argued that, in an unregulated international market, the gross inequality of bargaining power between workers and companies would lead to exploitation.

But this paper has shown that attempts to improve on market outcomes may have unforeseen tragic consequences. We saw how raising the wages of workers in international sweatshops might wind up penalizing the most vulnerable workers (those in the informal sectors of developing countries) by depressing their wages and reducing their job opportunities in the formal sector. . . . As we have seen, above-market wages paid to sweatshop workers may discourage further investment and so perpetuate high unemployment. In turn, the higher unemployment may weaken the bargaining power of workers vis-à-vis employers. Thus, such market imperfections seem to call for more reliance on market forces rather than less. Likewise, the experience of the newly industrialized East Asian economies suggests that the best cure for the ills of sweatshops is more sweatshops. But most of the well-intentioned policies proposed by critics and business ethicists are likely to have the opposite effect.

Where does this leave the international manager? If the preceding analysis is correct, then it follows that it is ethically acceptable to pay market wage rates in developing countries (and to provide employment conditions appropriate for the level of development). That holds true even if the wages pay less than so-called living wages or subsistence or even (conceivably) the local minimum wage. The appropriate test is not whether the wage reaches some predetermined standard but whether it is freely accepted by (reasonably) informed workers. The workers themselves are in the best position to judge whether the wages offered are superior to their next-best alternatives. (The same logic applies *mutatis mutandis* to workplace labor standards).

Indeed, not only is it ethically acceptable for a company to pay market wages, but it may be ethically unacceptable for it to pay wages that exceed market levels. That will be the case if the company's above-market wages set precedents for other international companies that raise labor costs to the point of discouraging foreign investment. Furthermore, companies may have a social responsibility to transcend their own narrow concern with protecting their brand image and to publicly defend a system that has improved the lot of millions of workers in developing countries.

NOTES

1. Joanna Ramey and Joyce Barrett, "Apparel's ethical dilemma," *Women's Wear Daily,* March 18, 1996.
2. Steven Greenhouse, "A crusader makes celebrities tremble," *New York Times,* June 18, 1996, B4.
3. Peter Jacobi in Martha Nichols, "Third-world families at work: Child labor or child care," *Harvard Business Review* (Jan.–Feb. 1993).
4. Thomas Donaldson, *Ethics of International Business* (New York: Oxford University Press, 1989), 98.
5. Richard De George, *Competing with Integrity in International Business* (New York: Oxford University Press, 1993), 79.
6. De George, *Competing with Integrity,* 356–57.
7. Donaldson, *Ethics of International Business,* 145.
8. Ibid., 101.
9. Ibid., 103.
10. World Bank, *World Development Report 1995. "Workers in an Integrating World Economy"* (New York: Oxford University Press, 1995), 77.
11. Donaldson, *Ethics of International Business,* 115.
12. De George, *Competing with Integrity,* 48.
13. Kenneth P. Hutchinson, "Third world growth," *Harvard Business Review* (Nov.–Dec. 1994).
14. Terry Collingsworth, J. William Goold, Pharis J. Harvey, "Time for a global New Deal," *Foreign Affairs,* Jan.–Feb. 1994, 8.

15. Tim Smith, "The power of business for human rights," *Business & Society Review* (January 1994): 36.
16. Jeffrey Ballinger, "The new free trade heel," *Harper's Magazine*, August 1992, 46–47. "As in many developing countries, Indonesia's minimum wage, . . . is less than poverty level." Nina Baker, "The hidden hands of Nike," *Oregonian*, August 9, 1992.
17. Robert B. Reich, "Escape from the global sweatshop; Capitalism's stake in uniting the workers of the world," *Washington Post*, May 22, 1994. Reich's test is intended to apply in developing countries "where democratic institutions are weak or absent."
18. Reich, "Escape from the global sweatshop."
19. Hutchinson, "Third world growth."
20. Robin Broad and John Cavanaugh, "Don't neglect the impoverished South," *Foreign Affairs*, December 22, 1995.
21. John Cavanagh and Robin Broad, "Global reach; workers fight the multinationals," *The Nation*, March 18, 1996, p. 21. See also Bob Herbert, "Nike's bad neighborhood," *New York Times*, June 14, 1996.
22. International Labor Organization, *World Employment 1995* (Geneva: ILO, 1995), 73.
23. World Bank, *Workers in an Integrating World Economy*, 5.
24. Keith B. Richburg, Anne Swardson, "U.S. industry overseas: Sweatshop or job source? Indonesians praise work at Nike factory," *Washington Post*, July 28, 1996.
25. Larry Rohter, "To U.S. critics, a sweatshop; for Hondurans, a better life," *New York Times*, July 18, 1996.
26. Marcus Brauchli, "Garment industry booms in Bangladesh," *Wall Street Journal*, August 6, 1991.
27. Lucy Martinez-Mont, "Sweatshops are better than no shops," *Wall Street Journal*, June 25, 1996.
28. Rohter, "To U.S. critics a sweatshop."
29. Richard J. Barnet and John Cavanagh, *Global Dreams* (New York: Simon & Schuster, 1994), 326.
30. William B. Falk, "Dirty little secrets," *Newsday*, June 16, 1996.
31. Barnet and Cavanagh, "Just undo it: Nike's exploited workers," *New York Times*, February 13, 1994.
32. ILO, *World Employment 1995*, 75.
33. World Bank, *The East Asian Miracle* (New York: Oxford University Press, 1993), 2.
34. Jagdish Bhagwati and Robert E. Hudec, eds., *Fair Trade and Harmonization* (Cambridge: MIT Press, 1996), vol. 1, p. 2.
35. World Bank, *Workers in an Integrating World Economy*, 75.

REVIEW AND DISCUSSION QUESTIONS

1. Explain why you agree or disagree with Maitland's characterization of the controversy over sweatshops as "the great non-debate." Do

you agree that the big companies that use sweatshops typically avoid debating the issue? If so, why do they avoid it?

2. What is Donaldson's test for determining whether wages and labor standards in sweatshops are morally appropriate? Are you persuaded by Maitland's criticism of Donaldson's test?

3. What is the classical liberal standard and why do Donaldson and De George find it inapplicable to poor developing countries? Explain why you agree or disagree with their arguments.

4. By American standards, wages in international sweatshops are very low, and working conditions appear terrible. Does the fact that foreign workers are eager to take these jobs establish that those wages and conditions are morally acceptable?

5. Critics of international sweatshops believe that their wages and working conditions are morally inadequate, that international sweatshops impoverish local workers and increase inequality between rich and poor, and that the companies that use them end up colluding with repressive regimes. Maitland disputes each of the points. With regard to each point, with whom do you agree and why?

6. Business ethicists such as Donaldson and De George believe that multinational companies operating in the third world should not leave it to the market alone to determine wages and working conditions. Maitland, to the contrary, argues that interfering with the market may have tragic consequences. With whom do you agree and why?

7. Maitland believes that international managers act rightly by paying market wages in developing countries and that it may even be wrong for them to pay wages that exceed market levels. What would you do if you were an international manager?

SUGGESTIONS FOR FURTHER READING

For more on ethics and international business, see Richard T. De George, "Ethical Dilemmas for Multinational Enterprise: A Philosophical Overview," in W. Michael Hoffman, Ann E. Lange, and David A. Fredo, eds., *Ethics and the Multinational Enterprise* (University Press of America 1986), Thomas Donaldson, "Values in Tension: Ethics Away from Home," *Harvard Business Review* 74 (September-October 1996), Norman E Bowie, "Relativism and the Moral Obligations of Multinational Corporations," in Tom L. Beauchamp and Norman E. Bowie, eds., *Ethical Theory and Business,* 6th ed. (Prentice-Hall 2001), and Douglass Cassel, "Human Rights and Business Responsibilities in the Global Marketplace," *Business Ethics Quarterly* 11 (April 2001). On the use of child labor in sweatshops, see Hugh D. Hindman and Charles G. Smith, "Cross-Cultural Ethics and the Child Labor Problem," *Journal of Business Ethics* 19 (March 1999).

CHAPTER FIVE

When Is "Everyone's Doing It" a Moral Justification?

Ronald M. Green

People often give "Everyone's doing it" as a justification for engaging in conduct that is undesirable but widespread. This is certainly true in business, where the actions of competitors can pose difficult choices for moral managers. When does the claim that "Everyone's doing it" provide a sound moral reason for following others' lead? In this essay, Ronald M. Green, professor of religion at Dartmouth College, proposes five conditions as a guide for determining when the existence of a prevalent but otherwise undesirable pattern of behavior provides a moral justification for engaging in such behavior ourselves. He then tests these conditions by applying them to a series of business cases.

THINGS TO CONSIDER

1. In what circumstances are people likely to try to justify their conduct by saying "Everyone's doing it"?
2. Restate in your own words the five conditions that Green identifies.
3. What's the moral difference between satisfying the first four conditions and satisfying the fifth?
4. Explain why in Case 1 the "Everyone's doing it" argument fails Green's conditions.
5. What is different about Case 1′″?
6. Why does the marketing of infant formula in third world nations raise a moral issue?

From *Business Ethics Quarterly* 1 (January 1991). Copyright © 1991 The Society for Business Ethics. Reprinted by permission. Notes omitted.

The fact that "Everyone's doing it" is frequently appealed to as a reason why people feel morally justified in acting in less than ideal ways. This is particularly true in business matters, where competitive pressures often conspire to make perfectly upright conduct seem difficult if not impossible. . . .

The "Everyone's doing it" claim usually arises when we encounter a more or less prevalent form of behavior that is morally undesirable because it involves a practice that, on balance, causes harms people would like to avoid. Although it is rare that literally "everyone else" is engaged in this behavior, the "Everyone's doing it" claim is meaningfully made whenever a practice is widespread enough to make one's own forbearing from this conduct seem pointless or needlessly self-destructive. . . . In the commercial sphere, practices of bribery, cheating, and deception are common examples. Other things being equal, we and others would prefer that no one act in these ways, but the practices are widespread and our failing to participate in them can cause us serious loss or injury.

In what follows I want to focus on the use of the "Everyone's doing it" claim as a *justification* for conduct. This is not the only way this claim is used in our moral discourse. Sometimes the fact that many others are engaging in a form of conduct is offered as proof that the conduct is not really harmful or undesirable. Prevalent patterns of behavior may be offered as evidence for differing moral intuitions on a matter of dispute, as when Catholic liberals point to the use of birth control by many faithful believers as evidence for error in the Church's official moral teaching. Or prevalent behavior may be offered as an evidence for the existence (or nonexistence) of some morally relevant convention, as when the widespread and open giving of gifts at the closing of business deals is taken as a sign that this behavior is not regarded as bribery. Sometimes, as well, the "Everyone's doing it" claim is used to mitigate punishment for admittedly wrongful behavior, as when people argue that the prevalence of a certain form of immoral conduct renders it unjust to single out any one person for punishment.

The specific employment of the "Everyone's doing it" claim on which I want to focus differs from these situations in that there is no question that the behavior at issue is generally harmful and, hence, morally undesirable. If others were not acting in this way, I would not seek to justify doing so myself. Nor am I merely seeking to avoid being singled out for punishment for wrongful past acts. Because others are acting in this undesirable way, and because I may suffer serious harm or loss if I do not follow their lead, the "Everyone's doing it" claim is made as a way of defending the moral permissibility of my (even prospectively) imitating their behavior.

Facing situations of this sort, where the prospect of injury or serious loss is present, I believe, the five conditions listed on the following table guide our thinking about when it is morally permissible to adopt an otherwise undesirable but prevalent practice ourselves. If all five of these conditions, or at least the first four, are met, it is morally permitted to act as others are doing. If any of the first four are not satisfied, we'll see, moral decision becomes more complex.

◆
---

*Conditions Permitting One to Engage in
Harmful but Prevalent Behavior*

1. Refraining from this behavior will unavoidably cause you (or those you care for or for whom you are responsible) serious harm or loss.

2. Your engaging in this behavior will not also cause significantly more harm or loss to others.

3. Your engaging in this behavior will not lead others to engage in it in ways that are equally or more harmful, *and this would be true if your engaging in this behavior were to become public knowledge.*

4. Your refraining from this behavior will not lead others to refrain from it, *and this would be true if your refraining from this behavior were to become public knowledge.*

5. Your refraining from this behavior will unavoidably lead others to engage in it in ways that are substantially more harmful than would have been the case had you chosen to engage in it yourself *and this would be true if your refraining from this behavior were to become public knowledge.*

The first four of these conditions constitute *prima facie* reasons for one's allowably acting as others are doing in situations of this kind. If all four conditions are met one may morally choose either to act or *not* act as others are doing. If these first four conditions are satisfied, one is not *required* to act as others are doing. For personal reasons or reasons of prudence, one may forbear from doing what these conditions morally permit. Similarly, these conditions say nothing about supererogatory behavior that seeks to resist moral compromise. Thus, although one who follows others' lead when these conditions are satisfied may do so without blame, depending on further considerations he or she may also be praiseworthy for choosing not to do so. Only the fifth condition carries us over into a realm of possible moral requiredness. If this condition is met and no other way reasonably exists to forestall the harm involved, I may be called on to do what "Everyone else is doing" and may be faulted if I refrain from doing so, although this will depend on the degree of harm my conduct helps prevent. In the ensuing discussion, I will explore none of these finer distinctions, but it is important to recognize that the first four conditions do not ordinarily identify mandatory behavior. So long as the fifth condition is not involved, individuals whose scruples lead them to object to any form of moral compromise may well choose not to act in ways these conditions otherwise allow them to do.

As we might expect, it is rare for all these conditions to be met and equally rare for all *not* to be met. Hence, moral decision in cases where others are acting in undesirable ways frequently requires us to balance condition against condition and to assess the harms identified by each condition. Although there is no magical solution to this balancing problem, a key requirement is impartiality in reasoning. This is a fundamental feature of the "moral point of view." It requires us to evaluate the harms created or avoided by our conduct independently of the knowledge of how they affect ourselves (or those we care for). In some cases, this will be an extraordinarily difficult task, compounded by the confusion of personal information and motives with impartial reasoning in any actual instance of choice. Nevertheless, these five conditions can at least preliminarily assist us in this complex process by identifying the morally relevant matters we must address.

Why are these considerations the important ones? We may think of them as arising out of and expressing the more basic logic of the moral reasoning process. In keeping with this logic, morality aims at minimizing the infliction of harm on persons against their will. Morality also seeks to provide a public forum of appeal concerning disputed modes of conduct. This means that moral choice, however private in fact, is always inherently public and requires us, at least in principle, to submit the rule implicit in our conduct to the approval of all persons it might affect. Finally, because of its public and rule-oriented character, moral reasoning supports conduct whose disclosure and expression as a public rule of allowable behavior would tend to discourage rather than encourage harmful behavior. Each of our five conditions is designed to express one or more aspects of this basic logic. The first and second conditions, for example, address the matter of proportionate harm. The third, fourth, and fifth conditions express our concern with the impact of our example on others' behavior, and the publicity clause in the third, fourth, and fifth conditions identifies the fact that it is the public rule implicit in our behavior that is morally relevant, not just the immediate impact of the behavior itself.

Do these conditions provide a complete and accurate guide to reasoning our way through "Everyone's doing it"–type situations? One way of answering this question is to see how thoroughly and well these conditions express the underlying logic of the moral reasoning process. A complementary approach is to see how well these conditions guide our thinking in specific cases of moral choice. In what follows, I want to take the second course, applying these conditions to a series of typical cases drawn from the business sector. If these conditions are consistently able to guide our thinking about complex choices in ways that correspond to, or at least do not seriously defy, our settled moral judgments about such matters, then we may assume that these conditions are an appropriate expression of the basic moral reasoning process applied to cases of this sort.

Case 1

You are the Philippines general manager of HAL, a large, multinational computer firm. Some months ago, the Philippine government placed an order for several of your firm's largest mainframe computers. The computers have arrived and are being held dockside by a regional office of the Customs Bureau. You learn that the reason for this delay is that a mid-level customs official is demanding a bribe to release the units for shipment. The sum involved is not large, but paying the bribe will violate HAL's policies and will require special authorization from the home office. You are reasonably confident that the payment is unnecessary. High officials in the government agencies who have ordered the units can soon be expected to bring pressure to bear on the Customs Bureau to have the units released. At worst, therefore, if you refuse to pay the bribe you face several more weeks of waiting. You know that bribery of customs officials is commonplace in the Philippines. May you appeal to this fact to expedite your shipment?

We have here a form of behavior that normally raises the "Everyone's doing it" claim. It is morally undesirable because it causes harm that, on balance, people would like to avoid, but it is nevertheless widely practiced. Bribery undermines economic rationality and stalls rather than expedites economic or political transactions. Nor is this a case of a harmless convention that only seems undesirable because of its unfamiliarity, for example, like the practice of petty "baksheesh" involving small payments to minor officials who earn their living this way in lieu of salaries. We may assume that the extortion involved here is substantial and genuinely impedes economic activity and development.

Despite the prevalence of this conduct in the Philippines your firm should not pay the bribe in this case because of the practice's undesirability and because not one of our five conditions is satisfied. Let's look at this in some detail, taking as our guide these five conditions expressed as a series of questions.

1. *Will refraining from bribery cause you (or those you care for or for whom you are responsible) serious and unavoidable harm or loss?*

For bribery to be justified in terms of this consideration, you must be able to answer this question "yes." However, in the case as described, the answer to this question seems to be "no." The harms and losses involved in not paying the bribe are minimal.

2. *Will your engaging in bribery also cause significantly more harm or loss to others?*

For bribery to be justified in terms of this consideration, the appropriate answer to this question is "no." This seems to be true, although, in view of the absence of harm to you or your firm in this case, the question itself does not seem applicable, as it would be in a case where harm to you had to be balanced against possible direct injury to others. If we think of the first of our five conditions as the driving force legitimating moral compromise, the failure to meet the first condition means that satisfying any of the restraining considerations represented by conditions 2 through 4 is morally irrelevant.

3. *Will your engaging in bribery lead others to engage in it in ways that are equally or more harmful,* and would this still be true if your engaging in bribery were to become public knowledge?

For bribery to be justified in terms of this consideration, the appropriate answer to this question must be "no." In this case, the answer is unclear. A large multinational firm's acquiescence to extortion of this sort may set an example for other firms, including many smaller and less powerful organizations. Furthermore, rewarding the extortionary activities of petty officials may encourage them to repeat this behavior in the future. This suggests an affirmative answer to the question. However, if we assume that bribery is already endemic in this environment, it may be reasonable to argue that one firm's conduct will have little or no impact on the prevalence of the practice. Note that because of the requirement that this encouragement not occur if this behavior were (even only hypothetically) to become public knowledge, this conclusion would hold even if the payment were made secretly.

4. *Will your refraining from bribery lead others to refrain from it,* and would this still be true if your refraining from bribery were to become public knowledge?

For bribery to be permissible in terms of this consideration, you must, again, be able to answer this question "no." As was true for the previous question, it is hard to determine whether a large multinational firm's decision actively to resist extortion of this sort will encourage others to follow its lead, although it is reasonable to suppose some effect of this sort. Corrupt customs officers may become more wary in the future about putting the squeeze on powerful multinational firms, especially if they find themselves subject to disciplinary action as a result. Hence, we can give a somewhat affirmative answer to this question, although the prevalence of this practice may mitigate the discouragement effect. Again, because of this condition's hypothetical requirement of publicity, this equivocal conclusion would hold even if HAL's resistance to extortion were not publicized in any way or if news of it were suppressed.

It is worth noting that the ways in which one's behavior encourages or discourages others' conduct are deliberately left unspecified in conditions 3 and 4. The wording "lead . . . to" is deliberately used so as to comprise both the effects of one's example on bystanders as well as the incentives created for others by one's conduct. As in law, reasonable and proximate causal pathways are assumed here rather than remote and unforeseeable events, although a diversity of such pathways must also be taken into account.

5. *Will your refraining from bribery unavoidably lead others to engage in it in ways that are substantially more harmful than would have been the case had you chosen to engage in it yourself* and would this still be true if your refraining from bribery were to become public knowledge?

There seems to be no reason to believe in this case that your refusing to pay the bribe will have this effect. Since a strongly affirmative answer is required here for complicity in this practice to be permissible (or required) this consideration lends no support to paying a bribe in this case.

Overall, although our second condition is not violated, none of the other conditions needed to justify acquiescence to extortion are clearly met in this case, and we can reasonably consider it morally impermissible to participate in this practice.

Case 1′

We can change this case slightly by invoking the possibility of serious harm to you, your firm, or the Philippine government as a result of a refusal to pay the bribe. Suppose, for example, that additional weeks of delay on the dock expose the computers to damage for which your division is financially responsible and which will seriously reduce profits. In that case, our first question receives the requisite affirmative answer: refusing to pay the bribe causes serious harm or loss, but this must still be weighed against the harm or stimulus to wrongdoing uncovered by our answers to the remaining four questions.

The second question is answered negatively, as it must be if paying the bribe is allowable in this case. You probably do not directly cause more harm to others than your firm is likely to suffer. However, the answers to questions 3, 4, and 5 remain the same as in the previous version of the case, and the possibly affirmative answers to 3 and 4, in particular, continue to provide good reasons for not paying the bribe. Although there is no simple formula for adjudicating the conflict here, these considerations suggest that even in the face of significant annoyance and injury, there is substantial moral reason for not acquiescing to extortion.

Case 1″

We can take this case one step farther and assume that at some point the harm incurred by resisting involvement in bribery increases significantly. This might be true, for example, if HAL's ability to do business in the Philippines were threatened by its refusal to pay bribes of this sort. Not only would this represent a substantial increment in the degree of harm experienced by the firm, but the fact that HAL's efforts are not supported by the government suggests that its refusal to engage in bribery is not significantly contributing to a reduction in bribery and extortion by others. Hence, condition 4 and (we may suppose) condition 3 are met in ways that increase the justifiability of involvement in this common but undesirable behavior.

Case 1‴

Finally, we might make one further change in the case to develop a far more compelling justification for involvement in bribery. Imagine, now, that instead of your firm's being a large and powerful multinational corporation, it is a small joint partnership whose economic survival depends on retaining a toehold in the Philippine market. Failure to pay the bribe in this case will represent economic disaster and loss for you and all the constituencies you represent.

Here we can give a strong affirmative answer to the first question. You suffer serious harm or loss if you refuse to pay the bribe. The second question is answered negatively as it must be for complicity to be allowable: no one is directly harmed by your bribery more than you and your firm are by not bribing. The third and fourth questions must also be answered negatively, and there is good reason to think that in this case they are. Given the pervasiveness of bribery and your firm's small size and lack of influence, paying or refusing to pay will likely have no impact on the prevalence of this behavior. Indeed, if you falter economically because of refusing to pay the bribe, other firms will surely step into your place and the practice will continue unabated. Although there is no suggestion here that your refusing to pay the bribe will accentuate the incidence or level of wrongdoing—and hence that condition 5 is met—the first four conditions are satisfied and, according to our conditions, bribery is morally permissible in this instance.

Of course, this is not the end of the matter. If it is true that the practice of bribery is generally undesirable, even though in this case you might be morally justified in participating in it, this does not relieve you of any moral obligation you might have, whether as a member of society generally or as a person in a specific social role with corresponding duties, to seek to abate the practice as a whole. To the extent that you have some kind of obligation to help prevent or reduce harm to others, for example, you are called on to speak out publicly against extortion and bribery and you should also perhaps join industry-wide or civic efforts at reform. It is not necessarily true that if you choose to do this you must also morally refrain from paying bribes until they are more effectively banned. If you become prominent in the anti-bribery effort, your continued payment of bribes may be tactically unwise and it may also be wrong if you deceive people and lead them to think you are resisting bribery and extortion. But it is not clear so long as you are open about your conduct that you are wrong in continuing to pay bribes when they are a condition of doing business in the country and our other conditions are met.

Case 2

You are Vice President, Corporate Communications, of a large food processing firm, one of whose principal products is infant formula. A large share of your firm's formula sales take place in third world nations in Africa, Latin America, and the Caribbean where, along with your competitors, you actively engage in promoting formula used among new mothers. You all sample heavily in village health centers and urban hospitals and rely on medical professionals and paraprofessionals to promote your product.

Within the past year, an important international protest movement has developed against these policies. Critics point out that even under the best conditions, breast feeding is superior to bottle feeding, both because of the balanced nutrition and antibodies it provides and because of its value in infant-mother bonding. Furthermore, they say, in the third world environment, bottle feeding can be very harmful because water supplies are often contaminated and women are too poor to afford the level of formula purchases needed for adequate infant nutrition. Critics blame your marketing practices for the epidemic of fatal newborn diarrhea in these regions and some have begun to use words like "genocide" to describe your conduct.

Infant formula sales overseas constitute roughly 25 percent of your firm's total revenues and, because of the return to breast feeding in the United States, are the fastest growing sector of its business. Shortly, you will participate in a meeting of your firm's Executive Committee where a strategy to respond to the rising tide of criticism will be discussed. At that meeting, you will be called on to articulate the moral issues involved here. You are aware that many persons in your firm believe that your conduct is ethical. Some feel you are making an option available to women in these countries they would not otherwise have. They point out that no one is being forced to adopt bottle feeding and that some women unable to nurse would be seriously harmed if you withdrew from the market. Finally, whatever their views on these other matters, many in your firm believe that if you were to withdraw from this business or to market less aggressively, nothing would be accomplished. Competitors (some based in other countries and not subject to U.S. laws or codes) would merely step into the void your departure creates. Those who argue this way concede that your present practices have probably contributed to the rise in infant mortality in the third world. But they see a change in policy as accomplishing nothing while economically damaging your firm.

Once again we have a case to which our five conditions are meant to apply. On balance, in its present form the marketing practices of infant formula firms are undesirable. Even if these practices have some beneficial aspects, they inflict unnecessary harm on many third world children. Nevertheless, "Everyone's doing it," in the sense that the practice is prevalent, and if your firm does not, others will. How would you answer each of the five relevant questions in this case?

1. *Will refraining from aggressive marketing of infant formula in the third world unavoidably cause your firm serious harm or loss?*

Assuming that third world sales represent a substantial and growing share of your company's business, and that all the relevant alternatives are even more costly for the firm, it seems that this question receives an affirmative answer. On this count, then, continuing your policy might be justifiable.

2. *Will your aggressive marketing of infant formula in the third world cause significantly more harm to others?*

I think the answer to this question is almost certainly "yes." If the critics are right—and for our purposes here we may assume they are—many thousands of third world children will die or be subject to the ravages of malnutrition as a direct result of your current marketing practices. Since few people would argue that profit considerations of this sort justify inflicting death and suffering on so many children, your conduct here seems morally unjustifiable.

Whichever way you answer questions 3 and 4 will only sustain or reinforce this judgment. If your continued marketing of formula this way encourages other firms to do so, then this conduct becomes even more unjustifiable, whereas its having no effect still leaves you directly involved in the imposition of disproportionate harm on children. If your refraining from these practices causes others to follow suit, this constitutes a further reason for altering your conduct, but even if this doesn't occur, ceasing this marketing would at least prevent your firm from being an agent of disproportionate harm to others.

Incidentally, we may think of this second condition as a kind of damper on the spread of disproportionately harmful behavior. Permitting people to engage in such behavior merely because others are (or inevitably will) do so and because the net balance of harm will remain unaffected if one withdraws is an open invitation to the proliferation of harmful conduct. This second condition rules out such complicity. Only if conditions 3, 4, and 5 are further satisfied—that is, if one's behavior does not encourage others to engage in it, if one's refraining would not discourage them, and if the net harm created by one's refraining from a practice can be shown to be unavoidably and substantially greater than one's engaging in it—may involvement in the infliction of direct, disproportionate harm be justified.

About the only way the case for continuing these practices could be made, therefore, is if condition 5 were met. This would require a strongly affirmative answer to the following question, *"Will your re-*

fraining from aggressive marketing of infant formula in the third world lead others to engage in it in ways that are substantially more harmful than would have been the case had you chosen to engage in it yourselves?" In the next case, we'll encounter a situation where there might arguably be an affirmative answer to this question, but nothing presented in this case suggests such an answer here. Thus, the condition implicit in this question is not satisfied and your current practices are probably morally unjustifiable. Only the first consideration of financial loss supports your continued involvement, and few people believe that this is a good enough reason to inflict suffering and death on children.

This suggests the need for an alternative strategy if your firm is to preserve any kind of involvement in this market. Earlier we saw that when an otherwise morally undesirable practice exists, we always have some measure of moral responsibility to discourage it. This is true even when the conditions for one's complicity in the practice are fully satisfied, but this responsibility is magnified by prudential considerations when these conditions prohibit our involvement. In the case at hand, this recommends a complex strategy for your firm: forthright alignment of your public position with that of the formula marketing critics and active involvement or leadership in international efforts to regulate marketing practices by *all* infant formula firms in the third world environment. . . .

Case 3

You are Vice President, Corporate Communications, of one of the largest brewing firms in the United States. Like most other large brewers in this country, your company engages in a substantial marketing effort aimed at the college age population. This effort has more than immediate sales as its object since studies show that brand preferences for beer are firmly established during the college years. In order to capture a large share of this important market, your firm, like its competitors, advertises heavily in college publications and national print and broadcast media aimed at college students. You also engage in substantial promotional activities on campuses where this is allowed. These range from matching grants for student-run charitable telethons and sports activities to "wet tee shirt contests" and other forms of social activity.

Recently, these practices have come under attack. Critics maintain they help create a "culture of alcohol" that has contributed to a dramatic rise of drinking problems among younger people. They point to the growing incidence of alcohol abuse on college campuses nationwide and to studies linking such abuse during the college years to alcoholism later in life. Some of these critics have called on brewers to eliminate these marketing activities voluntarily, while others have demanded an outright legal ban on these activities.

In an interview reported in the national press, the CEO of your company recently went on record as being concerned about these practices. Although he did not agree that alcohol abuse can be blamed on the availability or promotion of alcoholic beverages, he conceded that many of the promotional efforts you and your competitors engage in are "distasteful." He expressed the wish that the industry as a whole could somehow "get its act together" to improve its record in this area. But he added that without an industry-wide agreement, no single firm could withdraw from the college market. "As things now stand," he observed, "the college market is the name of the game." At the close of this interview, your CEO pointed out that the promotional activities of your firm are significantly better than most of its competitors. Your marketing people take special care to see that your campus-based activities involve only students of legal drinking age and are adequately supervised by responsible authorities. Your print and broadcast ads aimed at college students also stress moderation in the use of alcohol. Whenever practicable, print ads contain explicit warnings about the dangers of alcohol abuse. Finally, you have been committed for several years to devoting a significant portion (10 percent) of your marketing budget to the support of alcohol education programs on college campuses across the nation.

Not entirely satisfied with the course of this interview, your CEO subsequently designated a committee of senior officers to study alternatives for the company in this area. You are a member of that committee. As you would expect, the discussions have been vigorous. Some members have argued strongly that they see nothing wrong in current promotional activities. These are aimed, they maintain, at college age adults who should be free to make their own decisions in this area. One member of the committee summed up this view when he stated that "Prohibition is over."

Other members of the committee are less sure that your activities have not unintentionally contributed to problems of alcohol abuse on campus and beyond. They argue, however, that it would be pointless for your firm to withdraw from this market. Competitors would be eager to step in and assume the market share you lose. One committee member who argues this way goes farther: she contends that your withdrawing from this market will be morally counterproductive. "We are the most ethically responsible firm in this area," she insists. "Our ads and campus-based activities are not only responsible, they make a positive contribution to alcohol education. None of our competitors has shown equivalent responsibility. If we get out, college students will be the losers."

You are puzzled by this gamut of arguments. How do our five conditions bear on the issue? In view of the fact that college age students constitute such an important part of a brewer's market, there is probably no doubt that a unilateral withdrawal from these activities will financially damage your firm. Our first condition, therefore, seems reasonably satisfied in this case. The meaning of the second condition for this case is less clear. Although there is controversy over whether beer advertising and promotion contribute to alcohol abuse, even your CEO has expressed concern here by stating his belief that it would probably be better if all members of the industry showed more restraint.

The answers to the questions implicit in our third and fourth conditions are also less than clear. Does your firm's engaging in the gamut of its marketing activities contribute to other firms' following its lead? Would its publicly announced withdrawal from this market or specific marketing activities put pressure on leading competitors to follow suit? An argument can be made for positive answers to both questions, especially the second one. In view of the developing public reaction against these practices, a unilateral move by an industry leader might have a significant impact on industry-wide practice or on the legal environment.

In view of the opposing set of considerations exposed by a review of conditions 1 through 4, the fifth condition becomes especially important. To what extent will your firm's withdrawal from this market be a victory for personal moral purity gained at the expense of a real and adverse impact on college populations as a whole? Will your refraining from involvement in this area unavoidably cause a net and significant increase in irresponsible advertising and promotional activities by others who will step into the place your departure creates?

The answer to this question is itself unclear and probably cannot be determined apart from a specific investigation of the dynamics of this industry and the effect of your involvement *versus* that of others. Nevertheless, to this point, our analysis reveals several things. First, that the fifth condition may legitimately be introduced as a consideration in "Everyone's doing it"–type situations. Members of the committee who urge this matter are not wrong to do so and there will be situations when satisfying this condition will clearly justify complicity and continued involvement in less than ideal practices. This situation may not be one of them, however, and this illustrates a second point: that it is not enough to claim the applicability of condition 5. One must show that it is satisfied beyond reasonable doubt in order to justify involvement in practices markedly violating other conditions. It is thoroughly predictable that those engaged in prevalent but undesirable conduct will seek to justify their doing so on the grounds that others' involvement will somehow increase the net level of harm. In view of this, condition 5 must be thought to impose an especially severe constraint on decision makers: they must show beyond reasonable doubt that their continued involvement helps avoid a significant level of increased harm, and they must show that the harm avoided clearly outweighs any immediate harms and relevant encouragement or discouragement effects governed by conditions 2, 3, and 4.

Is this stern standard met in this case? I personally think it is not. I am not persuaded by the bare facts of this case that whatever positive effects result from this firm's college marketing program really offset the immediate injury inflicted on some college students by the stimulus to excessive alcohol consumption. Nor am I convinced that the powerful example of an industry leader publicly withdrawing from involvement in these activities, perhaps hand-in-hand with its assuming the role of leadership in an industry-wide drive for self-restraint, would not in the long run prove effective in reducing the harms associated with current practices.

The point here, however, is not to resolve this case, which involves complex factual matters beyond our reach, so much as it is to illustrate the way in which these five conditions focus discussion and inquiry. Frequently in the course of moral debate one or another of these conditions is appealed to, but often only in an implicit or oblique fashion that impedes thorough analysis. By taking these conditions separately, each condition may be given the degree of logical and factual examination appropriate to it in the case at hand. In this instance, for example, the potentially strongest argument in the firm's favor, its claim that its marketing activities relatively benefit college age students, seems less persuasive when brought to the fore and exposed to critical investigation than it does when it is an undifferentiated part of complex argument. This points up the value of analyzing an "Everyone's doing it" situation in terms of each of these five conditions. By proceeding carefully, condition by condition, we are better able to identify the facts and claims relevant to each aspect of what are usually complex arguments about a form of behavior.

Conclusion

The task of identifying a set of justifying conditions for complex cases of moral choice points in two different directions. On the one hand, these conditions must be shown to reflect and adequately express the relevant considerations governing all moral choice, what I earlier called the basic "logic" of the moral reasoning process. On the other hand, a list of justifying conditions must also adequately guide judgment through both familiar and novel cases for decision and it must do so without violating some of our firmest and most settled judgments about these cases. When these two sides of the task are adequately accomplished, we can say that an exercise of this sort is successful and that we are in a position of "reflective equilibrium" before the issues at hand.

The foregoing investigation sought only to accomplish a fragment of this task. Although I suggested the conformity of these five conditions to the basic logic of the moral reasoning process, I did not develop this point. Instead, I chose to focus on the second part of the task: applying these conditions to a series of complex cases. I have tried to suggest that these conditions furnish a useful guide to judgment. Showing this to be consistently true for all cases, using these conditions to assess and adequately respond to competing intuitions about concrete cases, and seeing if we can go beyond a listing of conditions to a more precise adjudication of conflicts among them are tasks that lie ahead. For now I hope we have made a beginning in addressing one of ethics' most persistent and puzzling questions.

REVIEW AND DISCUSSION QUESTIONS

1. How common do you think it is for people to try to justify their conduct by saying "Everyone's doing it"?
2. Assess Green's claim that his five conditions arise out of and express the basic logic of the moral reasoning process.
3. Carefully examine Case 1 and the three variations on it in light of Green's five conditions. Do you agree with the moral conclusions he draws? Does your assessment of these cases increase or decrease your confidence in Green's approach?
4. Do you agree with Green that in cases of morally permissible bribery, one may still have an obligation to combat the practice? If so, what would this imply in practical terms?
5. Under what circumstances, if any, would a firm be justified in marketing infant formula in a developing country?
6. Analyze the application of condition 5 to Case 3. Is it plausible to believe that it might justify the company's remaining in the college market?
7. In your view is drinking by college students a serious problem, or is the issue exaggerated? Do you believe that marketing helps to create a "culture of alcohol" on campus? If so, what does morality require the makers of beer, wine, and other alcoholic beverages to do?
8. Do you believe that Green's five conditions provide a useful framework for determining when "Everyone's doing it" provides a legitimate justification for engaging in conduct that is undesirable but widespread? Explain why or why not.

SUGGESTIONS FOR FURTHER READING

Two interesting essays that pertain to Green's theme are Gregory S. Kavka, "When Two 'Wrongs' Make a Right: An Essay on Business Ethics," *Journal of Business Ethics 2* (February 1983), and Jonathan Glover, "It Makes No Difference Whether or Not I Do It," *Proceedings of the Aristotelian Society,* suppl. vol. 49 (1975). On overseas bribery, see Thomas W. Dunfree and Thomas J. Donaldson, "Untangling the Corruption Knot: Global Bribery Viewed through the Lens of Integrative Social Contract Theory," in Norman E. Bowie, ed., *The Blackwell Guide to Business Ethics* (Blackwell 2002). On the marketing of infant formula, see Lisa H. Newton and David P. Schmidt, *Wake-Up Calls: Classic Cases in Business Ethics* (Wadsworth 1996), Chapter 3. On the marketing of malt liquor, see George G. Brenkert, "Marketing to Inner-City Blacks: Powermaster and Moral Responsibility," *Business Ethics Quarterly* 8 (January 1998).

◆

CHAPTER SIX

Some Paradoxes of Whistleblowing

Michael Davis

When is whistleblowing morally justified? In this essay, Michael Davis, professor of philosophy at the Illinois Institute of Technology, critiques the standard theory of justified whistleblowing, arguing that it leads to three paradoxes. In its place he advocates what he calls the *complicity theory*. In contrast to the standard theory, which is concerned with the obligation of the whistleblower to prevent harm, the complicity theory focuses on the whistleblower's obligation to avoid complicity in wrongdoing. Davis tests his theory against a classic case of whistleblowing, Roger Boisjoly's testimony before the congressional commission investigating the *Challenger* disaster. (As a senior engineer at Morton Thiokol, Boisjoly had recommended against launching the space shuttle *Challenger* because the temperature at the launch site had fallen below the safety range for the O-ring seals in the rocket boosters. Top management overrode the recommendation, and shortly after being launched the next day, the *Challenger* exploded, killing all seven members of its crew.)

THINGS TO CONSIDER

1. According to Davis, the police officer, the criminal informant, and the clerk who happens upon evidence of wrongdoing in another department are not whistleblowers. Why not?
2. According to the standard theory, when is whistleblowing morally permissible and when is it morally required?
3. Explain the paradox of burden, the paradox of missing harm, and the paradox of failure.
4. What are the main differences between Davis's complicity theory and the standard theory?

From *Business and Professional Ethics Journal* 15 (Spring 1996). Reprinted by permission of the author. Some notes omitted.

INTRODUCTION

By "paradox" I mean an apparent—and, in this case, real—inconsistency between theory (our systematic understanding of whistleblowing) and the facts (what we actually know, or think we know, about whistleblowing). What concerns me is not a few anomalies, the exceptions that test a rule, but a flood of exceptions that seems to swamp the rule.

This paper has four parts. The first states the standard theory of whistleblowing. The second argues that the standard theory is paradoxical, that it is inconsistent with what we know about whistleblowers. The third part sketches what seems to me a less paradoxical theory of whistleblowing. The fourth tests the new theory against one classic case of whistleblowing, Roger Boisjoly's testimony before the presidential commission investigating the *Challenger* disaster ("the Rogers Commission"). I use that case because the chief facts are both uncontroversial enough and well-known enough to make detailed exposition unnecessary. For the same reason, I also use that case to illustrate various claims about whistleblowing throughout the paper.

JUSTIFICATION AND WHISTLEBLOWING

The standard theory is not about whistleblowing, as such, but about justified whistleblowing—and rightly so. Whether this or that is, or is not, whistleblowing is a question for lexicographers. For the rest of us, mere moral agents, the question is—when, if ever, is whistleblowing justified?

We may distinguish three (related) senses in which an act may be "justified." First, an act may be something morality permits. Many acts, for example, eating fruit at lunch, are morally justified in this weak sense. They are (all things considered) morally all right, though some of the alternatives are morally all right too. Second, acts may be morally justified in a stronger sense. Not only is doing them morally all right, but doing anything else instead is morally wrong. These acts are *morally* required. Third, some acts, though only morally justified in the weaker sense, are still required all things considered. That is, they are mandatory because of some non-moral consideration. They are *rationally* (but not morally) required.

I shall be concerned here only with *moral* justification, that is, with what morality permits or requires. I shall have nothing to say about when other considerations, for example, individual prudence or social policy, make (morally permissible) whistleblowing something reason requires.

Generally, we do not *need* to justify an act unless we have reason to think it wrong (whether morally wrong or wrong in some other way). So, for example, I do not need to justify eating fruit for lunch today, though I would if I were allergic to fruit or had been keeping a fast. We also do not need a justification if we believe the act in question wrong. We do not need a justification because, insofar as an act is wrong, justification is impossible. The point of justification is to show to be right an act the rightness of which has been put in (reasonable) doubt. Insofar as we believe the act wrong, we can only condemn or excuse it. To condemn it is simply to declare it wrong. To excuse it is to show that, while the act was wrong, the doer had good reason to do it, could not help doing it, or for some other reason should not suffer the response otherwise reserved for such a wrongdoer.

Most acts, though permitted or required by morality, need no justification. There is no reason to think them wrong. Their justification is too plain for words. Why then is whistleblowing so problematic that we need *theories* of its justification? What reason do we have to think whistleblowing might be morally wrong?

Whistleblowing always involves revealing information that would not ordinarily be revealed. But there is nothing morally problematic about that; after all, revealing information not ordinarily revealed is one function of science. Whistleblowing always involves, in addition, an actual (or at least declared) intention to prevent something bad that would otherwise occur. There is nothing morally problematic in that either. That may well be the chief use of information.

What seems to make whistleblowing morally problematic is its organizational context. A mere individual cannot blow the whistle (in any interesting sense); only a member of an organization, whether a current or a former member, can do so. Indeed, he can only blow the whistle on his own organization (or some part of it). So, for example, a police officer who makes public information about a burglary ring, though a member of an organization, does not blow the whistle on the burglary ring (in any interesting sense). He simply alerts the public. Even if he came by the information working undercover in the ring, his revelation could not be whistleblowing. While secret agents, spies, and other infiltrators need a moral justification for what they do, the justification they need differs from that which whistleblowers need. Infiltrators gain their information under false pretenses. They need a justification for that deception. Whistleblowers generally do not gain their information under false pretenses.

What if, instead of being a police officer, the revealer of information about the burglary ring were an ordinary member of the ring? Would such an informer be a (justified) whistleblower? I think not. The burglary ring is a criminal organization. The whistleblower's organization never is, though it may occasionally engage in criminal activity (knowingly or inadvertently). So, even a burglar who, having a change of heart, volunteers information about his ring to the police or the newspaper, does not need to justify his act in the way the whistleblower does. Helping to destroy a criminal organization by revealing its secrets is morally much less problematic than whistleblowing.

What then is morally problematic about the whistleblower's organizational context? The whistleblower cannot blow the whistle using just any information obtained in virtue of membership in the organization. A clerk in Accounts who, happening upon evidence of serious wrongdoing while visiting a friend in Quality Control, is not a whistleblower just because she passes the information to a friend at the *Tribune*. She is more like a self-appointed spy. She seems to differ from the whistleblower, or at least from clear cases of the whistleblower, precisely in her relation to the information in question. To be a whistleblower is to reveal information with which one is *entrusted*.

But it is more than that. The whistleblower does not reveal the information to save his own skin (for example, to avoid perjury under oath). He has no excuse for revealing what his organization does not want revealed. Instead, he claims to be doing what he should be doing. If he cannot honestly make that claim—if, that is, he does not have that intention—his revelation is not whistleblowing (and so, not justified as whistleblowing), but something analogous, much as pulling a child from the water is not a rescue, even if it saves the child's life, when the "rescuer" merely believes herself to be salvaging old clothes. What makes whistleblowing morally problematic, if anything does, is this high-minded but unexcused misuse of one's position in a generally law-abiding, morally decent organization, an organization that *prima facie* deserves the whistleblower's loyalty (as a burglary ring does not).

The whistleblower must reveal information the organization does not want revealed. But, in any actual organization, "what the organization wants" will be contested, with various individuals or groups asking to be taken as speaking for the organization. Who, for example, did what Thiokol wanted the night before the *Challenger* exploded? In retrospect, it is obvious that the three vice presidents, Lund, Kilminster, and Mason, did not do what Thiokol wanted—or, at least, what it would have wanted. At the time, however, they had authority to speak for the company—the conglomerate Morton-Thiokol headquartered in Chicago—while the protesting engineers, including Boisjoly, did not. Yet, even before the explosion, was it obvious that the three were doing what the company wanted? To be a whistleblower, one must, I think, at least temporarily lose an argument about what the organization wants. The whistleblower is disloyal only in a sense—the sense the winners of the internal argument get to dictate. What can justify such disloyalty?

THE STANDARD THEORY

According to the theory now more or less standard,[1] such disloyalty is morally permissible when:

(S1) The organization to which the would-be whistleblower belongs will, through its product or policy, do serious considerable harm to the public (whether to users of its product, to innocent bystanders, or to the public at large);

(S2) The would-be whistleblower has identified that threat of harm, reported it to her immediate superior, making clear both the threat itself and the objection to it, and concluded that the superior will do nothing effective; and

(S3) The would-be whistleblower has exhausted other internal procedures within the organization (for example, by going up the organizational ladder as far as allowed)—or at least made use of as many internal procedures as the danger to others and her own safety make reasonable.

Whistleblowing is morally required (according to the standard theory) when, in addition:

(S4) The would-be whistleblower has (or has accessible) evidence that would convince a reasonable, impartial observer that her view of the threat is correct; and

(S5) The would-be whistleblower has good reason to believe that revealing the threat will (probably) prevent the harm at reasonable cost (all things considered).

Why is whistleblowing morally required when these five conditions are met? According to the standard theory, whistleblowing is morally required, when it is required at all, because "people have a moral obligation to prevent serious harm to others if they can do so with little cost to themselves."[2] In other words, whistleblowing meeting all five conditions is a form of "minimally decent Samaritanism" (a doing of what morality requires) rather than "good Samaritanism" (going well beyond the moral minimum). . . .

THREE PARADOXES

That's the standard theory—where are the paradoxes? The first paradox I want to call attention to concerns a commonplace of the whistleblowing literature. Whistleblowers are not minimally decent Samaritans. If they are Samaritans at all, they are good Samaritans. They always act at considerable risk to career, and generally, at considerable risk to their financial security and personal relations.[3]

In this respect, as in many others, Roger Boisjoly is typical. Boisjoly blew the whistle on his employer, Thiokol; he volunteered information, in public testimony before the Rogers Commission, that Thiokol did not want him to volunteer. As often happens, both his employer and many who relied on it for employment reacted hostilely. Boisjoly had to say goodbye to the company town, to old friends and neighbors, and to building rockets; he had to start a new career at an age when most people are preparing for retirement.

Since whistleblowing is generally costly to the whistleblower in some large way as this, the standard theory's minimally decent Samaritanism provides *no* justification for the central cases of whistleblowing.[4] That is the first paradox, what we might call "the paradox of burden."

The second paradox concerns the prevention of "harm." On the standard theory, the would-be whistleblower must seek to prevent "serious and considerable harm" in order for the whistleblowing to be even morally permissible. There seems to be a good deal of play in the term *harm*. The harm in question can be physical (such as death or disease), financial (such as loss of or damage to property), and perhaps even psychological (such as fear or mental illness). But there is a limit to how much the standard theory can stretch "harm." Beyond that limit are "harms" such as injustice, deception, and waste. As morally important as injustice, deception, and waste can be, they do not seem to constitute the "serious and considerable harm" that can require someone to become even a minimally decent Samaritan.

Yet, many cases of whistleblowing, perhaps most, are not about preventing serious and considerable physical, financial, or psychological harm. For example, when Boisjoly spoke up the evening before the *Challenger* exploded, the lives of seven astronauts sat in the balance. Speaking up then was about preventing serious and considerable physical, financial, and psychological harm—but it was not whistleblowing. Boisjoly was then serving his employer, not betraying a trust (even on the employer's understanding of that trust); he was calling his superiors' attention to what he thought they should take into account in their decision and not publicly revealing confidential information. The whistleblowing came after the explosion, in testimony before the Rogers Commission. By then, the seven astronauts were beyond help, the shuttle program was suspended, and any further threat of physical, financial, or psychological harm to the "public" was—after discounting for time—negligible. Boisjoly had little reason to believe his testimony would make a significant difference in the booster's redesign, in safety procedures in the shuttle program, or even in reawakening concern for safety among NASA employees and contractors. The *Challenger*'s explosion was much more likely to do that than anything Boisjoly could do. What Boisjoly could do in his testimony, what I think he tried to do, was prevent falsification of the record.

Falsification of the record is, of course, harm in a sense, especially a record as historically important as that which the Rogers Commission was to produce. But falsification is harm only in a sense that almost empties "harm" of its distinctive meaning, leaving it more or less equivalent to "moral wrong." The proponents of the standard theory mean more by "harm" than that. De George, for example, explicitly says that a threat justifying whistleblowing must be to "life or health."[5] The standard theory is strikingly more narrow in its grounds of justification than many examples of justified whistleblowing suggest it should be. That is the second paradox, the "paradox of missing harm."

The third paradox is related to the second. Insofar as whistleblowers are understood as people out to prevent harm, not just to prevent moral wrong, their chances of success are not good. Whistleblowers generally do not prevent much harm. In this too, Boisjoly is typical. As he has said many times, the situation at Thiokol is now much as it was before the disaster. Insofar as we can identify cause and effect, even now we have little reason to believe that—whatever his actual intention—Boisjoly's testimony actually prevented any harm (beyond the moral harm of falsification). So, if whistleblowers must have, as the standard theory says (S5), (beyond the moral wrong of falsification) "good reason to believe that revealing the threat will (probably) prevent the harm," then the history of whistleblowing virtually rules out the moral justification of whistleblowing. That is certainly paradoxical in a theory purporting to state sufficient conditions for the central cases of justified whistleblowing. Let us call this "the paradox of failure."

A COMPLICITY THEORY

As I look down the roll of whistleblowers, I do not see anyone who, like the clerk from Accounts, just happened upon key documents in a cover-up.[6] Few, if any, whistleblowers are mere third-parties like the good Samaritan. They are generally deeply involved in the activity they reveal. This involvement suggests that we might better understand what justifies (most) whistleblowing if we understand the whistleblower's obligation to derive from *complicity* in wrongdoing rather than from the ability to prevent harm.

Any complicity theory of justified whistleblowing has two obvious advantages over the standard theory. One is that (moral) complicity itself presupposes (moral) wrongdoing, not harm. So, a complicity justification automatically avoids the paradox of missing harm, fitting the facts of whistleblowing better than a theory that, like the standard one, emphasizes prevention of harm.

That is one obvious advantage of a complicity theory. The second advantage is that complicity invokes a more demanding obligation than the ability to prevent harm does. We are morally obliged to avoid doing moral wrongs. When, despite our best efforts, we nonetheless find ourselves engaged in some wrong, we have an obligation to do what we reasonably can to set things right. If, for example, I cause a traffic accident, I have a moral (and legal) obligation to call help, stay at the scene until help arrives, and render first aid (if I know how), even at substantial cost to myself and those to whom I owe my time, and even with little likelihood that anything I do will help much. Just as a complicity theory avoids the paradox of missing harm, it also avoids the paradox of burden.

What about the third paradox, the paradox of failure? I shall come to that, but only after remedying one disadvantage of the complicity theory. That disadvantage is obvious—we do not yet have such a theory, not even a sketch. Here, then, is the place to offer a sketch of such a theory.

Complicity Theory.

You are morally required to reveal what you know to the public (or to a suitable agent or representative of it) when:

- **(C1)** What you will reveal derives from your work for an organization;
- **(C2)** You are a voluntary member of that organization;
- **(C3)** You believe that the organization, though legitimate, is engaged in serious moral wrongdoing;
- **(C4)** You believe that your work for that organization will contribute (more or less directly) to the wrong if (but *not* only if) you do not publicly reveal what you know;
- **(C5)** You are justified in beliefs C3 and C4; and
- **(C6)** Beliefs C3 and C4 are true.

The complicity theory differs from the standard theory in several ways worth pointing out here. The first is that, according to C1, what the whistleblower reveals must derive from his work for the organization. This condition distinguishes the whistleblower from the spy (and the clerk in Accounts). The spy seeks out information in order to reveal it; the whistleblower learns it as a proper part of doing the job the organization has assigned him. The standard theory, in contrast, has nothing to say about how the whistleblower comes to know of the threat she reveals (S2). For the standard theory, spies are just another kind of whistleblower.

A second way in which the complicity theory differs from the standard theory is that the complicity theory (C2) explicitly requires the whistleblower to be a *voluntary* participant in the organization in question. Whistleblowing is not—according to the complicity theory—an activity in which slaves, prisoners, or other involuntary participants in an organization engage. In this way, the complicity theory makes explicit something implicit in the standard theory. The whistleblowers of the standard theory are generally "employees." Employees are voluntary participants in the organization employing them.

What explains this difference in explicitness? For the Samaritanism of the standard theory, the voluntariness of employment is extrinsic. What is crucial is the ability to prevent harm. For the complicity theory, however, the voluntariness is crucial. The obligations deriving from complicity seem to vary with the voluntariness of our participation in the wrongdoing. Consider, for example, a teller who helps a gang rob her bank because they have threatened to kill her if she does not; she does not have the same obligation to break off her association with the gang as someone who has freely joined it. The voluntariness of employment means that the would-be whistleblower's complicity will be more like that of one of the gang than like that of the conscripted teller.

A third way in which the complicity theory differs from the standard theory is that the complicity theory (C3) requires moral wrong, not harm, for justification. The wrong need not be a new event (as a harm must be if it is to be *prevented*). It might, for example, consist in no more than silence about facts necessary to correct a serious injustice.

The complicity theory (C3) does, however, follow the standard theory in requiring that the predicate of whistleblowing be "serious." Under the complicity theory, minor wrongdoing can no more justify whistleblowing than can minor harm under the standard theory. While organizational loyalty cannot forbid whistleblowing, it does forbid "tattling," that is, revealing minor wrongdoing.

A fourth way in which the complicity theory differs from the standard theory, the most important, is that the complicity theory (C4) requires that the whistleblower believe that her work will have contributed to the wrong in question if she does nothing, but it does *not* require that she believe that her revelation will prevent (or undo) the wrong. The complicity theory does not require any belief about what the whistleblowing can accomplish (beyond ending complicity in the wrong in question). The whistleblower reveals what she knows in order to prevent complicity in the wrong, not to prevent the wrong as such. She can prevent complicity (if there is any to prevent) simply by publicly revealing what she knows. The revelation itself breaks the bond of complicity, the secret partnership in wrongdoing, that makes her an accomplice in her organization's wrongdoing. The complicity theory thus avoids the third paradox, the paradox of failure, just as it avoided the other two.

The fifth difference between the complicity theory and the standard theory is closely related to the fourth. Because publicly revealing what one knows breaks the bond of complicity, the complicity theory does not require the whistleblower to have enough evidence to convince others of the wrong in question. Convincing others, or just being able to convince them, is not, as such, an element in the justification of whistleblowing.

The complicity theory does, however, require (C5) that the whistleblower be (epistemically) justified in believing both that his organization is engaged in wrongdoing and that he will contribute to that wrong unless he blows the whistle. Such (epistemic) justification may require substantial physical evidence (as the standard theory says) or just a good sense of how things work. The complicity theory does not share the standard theory's substantial evidential demand (S4).

In one respect, however, the complicity theory clearly requires more of the whistleblower than the standard theory does. The complicity theory's C6—combined with C5—requires not only that the whistleblower be *justified* in her beliefs about the organization's wrongdoing and her part in it, but also that she be *right* about them. If she is wrong about either the wrongdoing or her complicity, her revelation will not be justified whistleblowing. This consequence of C6 is, I think, not as surprising as it may seem. If the would-be whistleblower is wrong only about her own complicity, her revelation of actual wrongdoing will, being otherwise justified, merely fail to be justified *as whistleblowing* (much as a failed rescue, though justified as an attempt, cannot be justified as a rescue). If, however, she is wrong about the wrongdoing itself, her situation is more serious. Her belief that wrong is being done, though fully justified on the evidence available to her, cannot justify her disloyalty. All her justified belief can do is *excuse* her disloyalty. Insofar as she acted with good intentions and while exercising reasonable care, she is a victim of bad luck. Such bad luck will leave her with an obligation to apologize, to correct the record (for example, by publicly recanting the charges she publicly made), and otherwise to set things right.

The complicity theory says nothing on at least one matter about which the standard theory says much—going through channels before publicly revealing what one knows. But the two theories do not differ as much as this difference in emphasis suggests. If going through channels would suffice to prevent (or undo) the wrong, then it cannot be true (as C4 and C6 together require) that the would-be whistleblower's work will contribute to the wrong if she does not publicly reveal what she knows. Where, however, going through channels would *not* prevent (or undo) the wrong, there is no need to go through channels. Condition C4's if-clause will be satisfied. For the complicity theory, going through channels is a way of finding out what the organization will do, not an independent requirement of justification. That, I think, is also how the standard theory understands it.[7]

A last difference between the two theories worth mention here is that the complicity theory is only a theory of morally required whistleblowing while the standard theory claims as well to define circumstances when whistleblowing is morally permissible but not morally required. This difference is another advantage that the complicity theory has over the standard theory. The standard theory, as we saw, has trouble making good on its claim to explain how whistleblowing can be morally permissible without being morally required.

TESTING THE THEORY

Let us now test the theory against Boisjoly's testimony before the Rogers Commission. Recall that under the standard theory any justification of that testimony seemed to fail for at least three reasons: First, Boisjoly could not testify without substantial cost to himself and Thiokol (to whom he owed loyalty). Second, there was no serious and substantial harm his testimony could prevent. And, third, he had little reason to believe that, even if he could identify a serious and considerable harm to prevent, his testimony had a significant chance of preventing it.

Since few doubt that Boisjoly's testimony before the Rogers Commission constitutes justified whistleblowing, if anything does, we should welcome a theory that—unlike the standard one—justifies that testimony as whistleblowing. The complicity theory sketched above does that:

(C1) Boisjoly's testimony consisted almost entirely of information derived from his work on booster rockets at Thiokol.

(C2) Boisjoly was a voluntary member of Thiokol.

(C3) Boisjoly believed Thiokol, a legitimate organization, was attempting to mislead its client, the government, about the causes of a deadly accident. Attempting to do that certainly seems a serious moral wrong.

(C4) On the evening before the *Challenger* exploded, Boisjoly gave up objecting to the launch once his superiors, including the three Thiokol vice presidents, had made it clear that they were no longer willing to listen to him. He also had a part in preparing those superiors to testify intelligently before the Rogers Commission concerning the booster's fatal field joint. Boisjoly believed that Thiokol would use his failure to offer his own interpretation of his retreat into silence the night before the launch, and the knowledge that he had imparted to his superiors, to contribute to the attempt to mislead Thiokol's client.

(C5) The evidence justifying beliefs C3 and C4 consisted of comments of various officers of Thiokol, what Boisjoly had seen at Thiokol over the years, and what he learned about the rocket business over a long career. I find this evidence sufficient to justify his belief both that his organization was engaged in wrong-doing and that his work was implicated.

(C6) Here we reach a paradox of *knowledge*. Since belief is knowledge if, but only if, it is *both* justified *and* true, we cannot *show* that we know anything. All we can show is that a belief is now justified and that we have no reason to expect anything to turn up later to prove it false. The evidence now available still justifies Boisjoly's belief both about what Thiokol was attempting and about what would have been his part in the attempt. Since new evidence is unlikely, his testimony seems to satisfy C6 just as it satisfied the complicity theory's other five conditions.

Since the complicity theory explains why Boisjoly's testimony before the Rogers Commission was morally required whistleblowing, it has passed its first test, a test the standard theory failed.

NOTES

1. Throughout this paper, I take the standard theory to be Richard T. De George's version in *Business Ethics*, 3rd Edition (New York: Macmillan, 1990), 200–14 (amended only insofar as necessary to include non-businesses as well as businesses). Why treat De George's theory as standard? There are two reasons: first, it seems the most commonly cited; and second, people offering alternatives generally treat it as the one to be replaced. The only obvious competitor, Norman Bowie's account, is distinguishable from De George's on no point relevant here. See Bowie's *Business Ethics* (Englewood Cliffs, NJ: Prentice-Hall, 1982), 143.

2. De George, *op. cit.*

3. For an explanation of why whistleblowing is inevitably a high risk undertaking, see my "Avoiding the Tragedy of Whistleblowing," *Business and Professional Ethics Journal* 8, no. 4 (1989): 3–19.

4. Indeed, I am tempted to go further and claim that, where an informant takes little or no risk, we are unlikely to describe her as a whistleblower at all. So, for example, I would say that using an internal or external "hot-line" is whistleblowing only when it is risky. We are, in other words, likely to consider using a hot-line as disloyalty (that is, as "going out of channels") only if the organization (or some part of it) is likely to respond with considerable hostility to its use.

5. De George, 210: "The notion of *serious* harm might be expanded to include serious financial harm, and kinds of harm other than death and serious threats to health and body. But as we noted earlier, we shall restrict ourselves here to products and practices that produce or threaten serious harm or danger to life and health."

6. See Myron Peretz Glazer and Penina Migdal Glazer, *The Whistleblowers: Exposing Corruption in Government and Industry* (New York: Basic Books, 1989) for a good list of whistleblowers (with detailed description of each); for an older list (with descriptions), see Alan F. Westin, *Whistleblowing! Loyalty and Dissent in the Corporation* (New York: McGraw-Hill, 1981).

7. Compare De George, 211: "By reporting one's concern to one's immediate superior or other appropriate person, one preserves and observes the regular practices of firms, which on the whole promote their order and efficiency; this fulfills one's obligation of minimizing harm, and *it precludes precipitous whistle blowing*." (Italics mine)

REVIEW AND DISCUSSION QUESTIONS

1. Most things we do require no justification. What makes whistle-blowing morally problematic—that is, why does it require justification in the first place?
2. Critically examine conditions S1 through S5 of the standard theory. Do you see any problems with them?
3. Davis argues that the standard theory gives rise to three paradoxes. Do they pose serious problems for the standard theory? For each of the alleged paradoxes, is there some way for a defender of the standard theory to respond to Davis's argument?
4. Explain the key features of Davis's theory of justified whistleblowing. Is his complicity theory an improvement over the standard theory? Explain why or why not.
5. Does the example of Roger Boisjoly fit the complicity theory better than it does the standard theory? If so, is this a conclusive reason for accepting the complicity theory? Are there examples of whistle-blowing that favor the standard theory over the complicity theory?
6. Are there any aspects of whistleblowing that Davis's theory neglects or fails to do full justice to?

SUGGESTIONS FOR FURTHER READING

Richard T. De George originally presented his criteria for assessing whistleblowing in "Ethical Responsibilities of Engineers in Large Organizations," *Business and Professional Ethics Journal* 1 (Fall 1981). Subsequent versions can be found in the different editions of his book *Business Ethics* (Prentice Hall). Gene G. James discusses De George's theory in "Whistle Blowing: Its Moral Justification," in W. Michael Hoffman, Robert E. Frederick, and Mark S. Schwartz, eds., *Business Ethics: Readings and Cases in Corporate Morality,* 4th ed. (McGraw-Hill 2001). Other good studies of the moral complexity of whistle-blowing are Michael Davis, "Avoiding the Tragedy of Whistleblowing," *Business and Professional Ethics Journal* 8 (Winter 1989), Natalie Dandekar, "Can Whistleblowing Be Fully Legitimated?" *Business and Professional Ethics Journal* 10 (Fall 1990), and Mike W. Martin, "Whistle-blowing: Professionalism, Personal Life, and Shared Responsibility for Safety in Engineering," *Business and Professional Ethics Journal* 11 (Summer 1992).

CHAPTER SEVEN

◆

Drug Testing in Employment

Joseph R. DesJardins and Ronald Duska

According to philosophy professors Joseph R. DesJardins (College of St. Benedict) and Ronald Duska (American College), privacy is an employee right, and drug testing is compatible with this right only if the information it seeks is relevant to the employment contract. DesJardins and Duska then critically assess two arguments intended to establish that knowledge of drug use is job-relevant information: first, that drug use adversely affects employee performance and, second, that it can harm the employer, other employees, and the public. Although they reject the first argument, they grant that, in certain limited circumstances, the second argument can justify drug testing. But even in these cases, strict procedural limitations should be placed on drug testing—despite the fact that drug use is illegal. They conclude by asking whether employee consent to drug testing is voluntary.

THINGS TO CONSIDER

1. According to DesJardins and Duska, when or under what circumstances does it violate an employee's right to privacy for an employer to request, collect, or use personal information?
2. Explain their criticisms of the argument that the information obtained by drug testing is job relevant (and therefore drug testing is permissible) because drug use adversely affects job performance.
3. DesJardins and Duska agree that drug testing can prevent harm and, thus, that the knowledge it provides is job relevant. Nevertheless, there are limits to this defense of drug testing. What are those limits?
4. Why is there a problem about the voluntariness of employee consent?

Originally published in *Business and Professional Ethics Journal,* Vol. 6, No. 3. Reprinted by permission of the authors from Joseph R. DesJardins and John J. McCall, eds., *Contemporary Issues in Business Ethics,* 4th ed. (Belmont, CA: Wadsworth, 2000). Notes abridged.

We take privacy to be an "employee right," by which we mean a presumptive moral entitlement to receive certain goods or be protected from certain harms in the workplace.[1] Such a right creates a prima facie obligation on the part of the employer to provide the relevant goods or, as in this case, refrain from the relevant harmful treatment. These rights prevent employees from being placed in the fundamentally coercive position where they must choose between their jobs and other basic human goods.

Further, we view the employer-employee relationship as essentially contractual. The employer-employee relationship is an economic one and, unlike relationships such as those between a government and its citizens or a parent and a child, exists primarily as a means for satisfying the economic interests of the contracting parties. The obligations that each party incurs are only those that it voluntarily takes on. Given such a contractual relationship, certain areas of the employee's life remain his or her own private concern, and no employer has a right to invade them. On these presumptions we maintain that certain information about an employee is rightfully private, in other words, that the employee has a right to privacy.

THE RIGHT TO PRIVACY

George Brenkert has described the right to privacy as involving a three-place relation between a person A, some information X, and another person B. The right to privacy is violated only when B deliberately comes to possess information X about A and no relationship between A and B exists that would justify B's coming to know X about A.[2] Thus, for example, the relationship one has with a mortgage company would justify that company's coming to know about one's salary, but the relationship one has with a neighbor does not justify the neighbor's coming to know that information.

Hence, an employee's right to privacy is violated whenever personal information is requested, collected, or used by an employer in a way or for any purpose that is *irrelevant to* or *in violation of* the contractual relationship that exists between employer and employee.

Since drug testing is a means for obtaining information, the information sought must be relevant to the contract if the drug testing is not to violate privacy. Hence, we must first decide whether knowledge of drug use obtained by drug testing is job relevant. In cases in which the knowledge of drug use is *not* relevant, there appears to be no justification for subjecting employees to drug tests. In cases in which information of drug use is job relevant, we need to consider if, when, and under what conditions using a means such as drug testing to obtain that knowledge is justified.

IS KNOWLEDGE OF DRUG USE JOB-RELEVANT INFORMATION?

Two arguments are used to establish that knowledge of drug use is job-relevant information. The first argument claims that drug use adversely affects job performance, thereby leading to lower productivity, higher costs, and consequently lower profits. Drug testing is seen as a way of avoiding these adverse effects. According to some estimates $25 billion are lost each year in the United States through loss in productivity, theft, higher rates in health and liability insurance, and similar costs incurred because of drug use.[3] Since employers are contracting with an employee for the performance of specific tasks, employers seem to have a legitimate claim upon whatever personal information is relevant to an employee's ability to do the job.

The second argument claims that drug use has been and can be responsible for considerable harm to individual employees, to their fellow employees, and to the employer, and third parties, including consumers. In this case drug testing is defended because it is seen as a way of preventing possible harm. Further, since employers can be held liable for harms done to employees and customers, knowledge of employee drug use is needed so that employers can protect themselves from risks related to such liability. But how good are these arguments?

THE FIRST ARGUMENT: JOB PERFORMANCE AND KNOWLEDGE OF DRUG USE

The first argument holds that drug use lowers productivity and that, consequently, an awareness of drug use obtained through drug testing will allow an employer to maintain or increase productivity. It is generally assumed that the performance of people using certain drugs is detrimentally affected by such use, and any use of drugs that reduces productivity is consequently job relevant: If knowledge of such drug use allows the employer to eliminate production losses, such knowledge is job relevant.

On the surface this argument seems reasonable. Obviously some drug use, in lowering the level of performance, can decrease productivity. Since the employer is entitled to a certain level of performance and drug use adversely affects performance, knowledge of that use seems job relevant.

But this formulation of the argument leaves an important question unanswered. To what level of performance are employers entitled? Optimal performance, or some lower level? If some lower level, what? Employers have a valid claim upon some *certain level* of performance, such that a failure to perform at this level would give the employer a justification for disciplining, firing, or at least finding fault with the employee. But that does not necessarily mean that the employer has a right to a maximum or optimal level of performance, a level above and beyond a certain level of acceptability. It might be nice if the employee gives an employer a maximum effort or optimal performance, but that is above and beyond the call of the employee's duty and the employer can hardly claim a right at all times to the highest level of performance of which an employee is capable. . . .

If the person is producing what is expected, knowledge of drug use on the grounds of production is irrelevant since, by this hypothesis, the production is satisfactory. If, on the other hand, the performance suffers, then to the extent that it slips below the level justifiably expected, the employer has preliminary grounds for warning, disciplining, or releasing the employee. But the justification for this action is the person's unsatisfactory performance, not the person's use of drugs. Accordingly, drug use information is either unnecessary or irrelevant and consequently there are not sufficient grounds to override the right of privacy. Thus, unless we can argue that an employer is entitled to optimal performance, the argument fails.

This counterargument should make it clear that the information that is job relevant, and consequently is not rightfully private, is information about an employee's level of performance and not information about the underlying causes of that level. The fallacy of the argument that promotes drug testing in the name of increased productivity is the assumption that each employee is obliged to perform at an optimal or at least quite high level. But this is required under few if any contracts. What is required contractually is meeting the normally expected levels of production or performing the tasks in the job description adequately (not optimally). If one can do that under the influence of drugs, then on the grounds of job performance at least, drug use is rightfully private. An employee who cannot perform the task adequately is not fulfilling the contract, and knowledge of the cause of the failure to perform is irrelevant on the contractual model.

Of course, if the employer suspects drug use or abuse as the cause of the unsatisfactory performance, then she might choose to help the person with counseling or rehabilitation. However, this does not seem to be something morally required of the employer. Rather, in the case of unsatisfactory performance, the employer has a prima facie justification for dismissing or disciplining the employee. . . .

THE SECOND ARGUMENT: HARM AND THE KNOWLEDGE OF DRUG USE TO PREVENT HARM

The performance argument is inadequate, but there is an argument that seems somewhat stronger. This is an argument that takes into account the fact that drug use often leads to harm. Using a variant of the Millian argument, which allows interference with a person's rights in order to prevent harm, we could argue that drug testing might be justified if such testing led to knowledge that would enable an employer to prevent harm.

Drug use certainly can lead to harming others. Consequently, if knowledge of such drug use can prevent harm, then knowing whether or not an employee uses drugs might be a legitimate concern of an employer in certain circumstances. This second argument claims that knowledge of the employee's drug use is job relevant because employees who are under the influence of drugs can pose a threat to the health and safety of themselves and others, and an employer who knows of that drug use and the harm it can cause has a responsibility to prevent it.

Employers have both a general duty to prevent harm and the specific responsibility for harms done by their employees. Such responsibilities are sufficient reason for any employer to claim that information about an employee's drug use is relevant if that knowledge can prevent harm by giving the employer grounds for dismissing the employee or not allowing him or her to perform potentially harmful tasks. Employers might even claim a right to reduce unreasonable risks, in this case the risks involving legal and economic liability for harms caused by employees under the influence of drugs, as further justification for knowing about employee drug use.

This second argument differs from the first, in which only a lowered job performance was relevant information. In this case, even to allow the performance is problematic, for the performance itself, more than being inadequate, can hurt people. We cannot be as sanguine about the prevention of harm as we can about inadequate production. Where drug use may cause serious harm, knowledge of that use becomes relevant if the knowledge of such use can lead to the prevention of harm and drug testing becomes justified as a means for obtaining that knowledge.

Jobs with Potential to Cause Harm

In the first place, it is not clear that every job has a potential to cause harm—at least, not a potential to cause harm sufficient to override a prima facie right to privacy. To say that employers can use drug testing where that can prevent harm is not to say that every employer has the right to know about the drug use of every employee. Not every job poses a threat serious enough to justify an employer coming to know this information.

In deciding which jobs pose serious-enough threats, certain guidelines should be followed. First the potential for harm should be *clear* and *present*. Perhaps all jobs in some extended way pose potential threats to human well-being. We suppose an accountant's error could pose a threat of harm to someone somewhere. But some jobs—such as those of airline pilots, school bus drivers, public transit drivers, and surgeons—are jobs in which unsatisfactory performance poses a clear and present danger to others. It would be much harder to make an argument that job performances by auditors, secretaries, executive vice-presidents for public relations, college teachers, professional athletes, and the like could cause harm if those performances were carried on under the influence of drugs. They would cause harm only in exceptional cases.[4]

Not Every Person Is to Be Tested

But, even if we can make a case that a particular job involves a clear and present danger for causing harm if performed under the influence of drugs, it is not appropriate to treat everyone holding such a job the same. Not every jobholder is equally threatening. There is less reason to investigate an airline pilot for drug use if that pilot has a twenty-year record of exceptional service than there is to investigate a pilot whose behavior has become erratic and unreliable recently, or one who reports to work smelling of alcohol and slurring his words. Presuming that every airline pilot is equally threatening is to deny individuals the respect that they deserve as autonomous, rational agents. It is to ignore their history and the significant differences between them. It is also probably inefficient and leads to the lowering of morale. It is the likelihood of causing harm, and not the fact of being an airline pilot per se, that is relevant in deciding which employees in critical jobs to test.

So, even if knowledge of drug use is justifiable to prevent harm, we must be careful to limit this justification to a range of jobs and people where the potential for harm is clear and present. The jobs must be jobs that clearly can cause harm, and the specific employee should not be someone who has a history of reliability. Finally, the drugs being tested should be those drugs that have genuine potential for harm if used in the jobs in question.

LIMITATIONS ON DRUG-TESTING POLICIES

Even when we identify those situations in which knowledge of drug use would be job relevant, we still need to examine whether some procedural limitations should not be placed upon the employer's testing for drugs. We have said when a real threat of harm exists and when evidence exists suggesting that a particular employee poses such a threat, an employer could be justified in knowing about drug use in order to prevent the potential harm. But we need to recognize that so long as the employer has the discretion for deciding when the potential for harm is clear and present, and for deciding which employees pose the threat of harm, the possibility of abuse is great. Thus, some policy limiting the employer's power is called for.

Just as criminal law imposes numerous restrictions protecting individual dignity and liberty on the state's pursuit of its goals, so we should expect that some restrictions be placed on employers to protect innocent employees from harm (including loss of job and damage to one's personal and professional reputation). Thus, some system of checks upon an employer's discretion in these matters seems advisable.

A drug-testing policy that requires all employees to submit to a drug test or to jeopardize their jobs would seem coercive and therefore unacceptable. Being placed in such a fundamentally coercive position of having to choose between one's job and one's privacy does not provide the conditions for a truly free consent. Policies that are unilaterally established by employers would likewise be unacceptable. Working with employees to develop company policy seems the only way to ensure that the policy will be fair to both parties. Prior notice of testing would also be required in order to give employees the option of freely refraining from drug use. Preventing drug use is morally preferable to punishing users after the fact, because this approach treats employees as capable of making rational and informed decisions.

Further procedural limitations seem advisable as well. Employees should be notified of the results of the test, they should be entitled to appeal the results (perhaps through further tests by an independent laboratory), and the information obtained through tests ought to be kept confidential. In summary, limitations upon employer discretion for administering drug tests can be derived from the nature of the employment contract and from the recognition that drug testing is justified by the desire to prevent harm, not the desire to punish wrongdoing.

THE ILLEGALITY CONTENTION

At this point critics might note that the behavior which testing would try to deter is, after all, illegal. Surely this excuses any responsible employer from being overprotective of an employee's rights. The fact that an employee is doing something illegal should give the employer a right to that information about his or her private life. Thus, it is not simply that drug use might pose a threat of harm to others, but that it is an *illegal* activity that threatens others. But again, we would argue that illegal activity itself is irrelevant to job performance. At best, *conviction* records might be relevant, but since drug tests are administered by private employers we are not only ignoring the question of conviction, we are also ignoring the fact that the employee has not even been arrested for the alleged illegal activity.

Further, even if the due process protections and the establishment of guilt are acknowledged, it still does not follow that employers have a claim to know about all illegal activity on the part of their employees.

Consider the following example: Suppose you were hiring an auditor whose job required certifying the integrity of your firm's tax and financial records. Certainly, the personal integrity of this employee is vital to adequate job performance. Would we allow the employer to conduct, with or without the employee's consent, an audit of the employee's own personal tax return? Certainly if we discover that this person has cheated on a personal tax return we will have evidence of illegal activity that is relevant to this person's ability to do the job. Given one's own legal liability for filing falsified statements, the employee's illegal activity also poses a threat to others. But surely, allowing private individuals to audit an employee's tax returns is too intrusive a means for discovering information about that employee's integrity. The government certainly would never allow this violation of an employee's privacy. It ought not to allow drug testing on the same grounds. Why tax returns should be protected in ways that urine, for example, is not, raises interesting questions of fairness. Unfortunately, this question would take us beyond the scope of this paper.

VOLUNTARINESS

A final problem that we also leave undeveloped concerns the voluntariness of employee consent. For most employees, being given the choice between submitting to a drug test and risking one's job by refusing an employer's request is not much of a decision at all. We believe that such decisions are less than voluntary and thereby hold that employers cannot escape our criticisms simply by including within the employment contract a drug-testing clause. Furthermore, there is reason to believe that those most in need of job security will be those most likely to be subjected to drug testing. Highly skilled, professional employees with high job mobility and security will be in a stronger position to resist such intrusions than will less skilled, easily replaced workers. This is why we should not anticipate surgeons and airline pilots being tested and should not be surprised when public transit and factory workers are. A serious question of fairness arises here as well.

Drug use and drug testing seem to be our most recent social "crisis." Politicians, the media, and employers expend a great deal of time and effort addressing this crisis. Yet, unquestionably, more lives, health, and money are lost each year to alcohol abuse than to marijuana, cocaine, and other controlled substances. We are well advised to be careful in considering issues that arise from such selective social concern. We will let other social commentators speculate on the reasons why drug use has received scrutiny while other white-collar crimes and alcohol abuse are ignored. Our only concern at this point is that such selective prosecution suggests an arbitrariness that should alert us to questions of fairness and justice.

In summary, then, we have seen that drug use is not always job relevant, and if drug use is not job relevant, information about it is certainly not job relevant. In the case of performance it may be a cause of some decreased performance, but it is the performance itself that is relevant to an employee's position, not what prohibits or enables that employee to do the job. In the case of potential harm being done by an employee under the influence of drugs, the drug use seems job relevant, and in this case drug testing to prevent harm might be legitimate. But how this is practicable is another question. It would seem that standard motor dexterity or mental dexterity tests given immediately prior to job performance are more effective in preventing harm, unless one concludes that drug use invariably and necessarily leads to harm. One must trust the individuals in any system for that system to work. One cannot police everything. Random testing might enable an employer to find drug users and to weed out the few to forestall possible future harm, but are the harms prevented sufficient to override the rights of privacy of the people who are innocent and to overcome the possible abuses we have mentioned? It seems not.

Clearly, a better method is to develop safety checks immediately prior to the performance of a job. Have a surgeon or a pilot or a bus driver pass a few reasoning and motor-skill tests before work. The cause of the lack of a skill, which lack might lead to harm, is really a secondary issue.

NOTES

1. "A Defense of Employee Rights," Joseph DesJardins and John McCall, *Journal of Business Ethics* 4 (1985). We should emphasize that our concern is with the *moral* rights of privacy for employees and not with any specific or prospective *legal* rights. . . .
2. "Privacy, Polygraphs, and Work," George Brenkert, *Journal of Business and Pro-*

fessional Ethics 1, no. 1 (Fall 1981). For a more general discussion of privacy in the workplace see "Privacy in Employment" by Joseph DesJardins, in *Moral Rights in the Workplace*, edited by Gertrude Ezorsky (Albany: SUNY Press, 1987). A good resource for philosophical work on privacy can be found in "Recent Work on the Concept of Privacy" by W.A. Parent, in *American Philosophical Quarterly* 20 (Oct. 1983): 341–58.

3. *U.S. News and World Report,* 22 Aug. 1983; *Newsweek,* 6 May 1983.
4. Obviously we are speaking here of harms that go beyond the simple economic harm that results from unsatisfactory job performance. These economic harms are discussed in the first argument above. Further, we ignore such "harms" as providing bad role models for adolescents, harms often used to justify drug tests for professional athletes. We think it unreasonable to hold an individual responsible for the image he or she provides to others.

REVIEW AND DISCUSSION QUESTIONS

1. Is the employer-employee relationship "essentially contractual"? If it is, what are the implications of this for business ethics?
2. Is privacy an employee right? Explain why or why not. If it is a right, give examples of employer actions or policies that would violate this right.
3. Do you agree that the central question regarding drug testing in employment is whether the information sought is job relevant? Are there other reasons for drug testing that don't turn on this issue?
4. Are you persuaded by DesJardins and Duska's reasons for rejecting the job-performance argument for drug testing? Explain why or why not.
5. How serious is the danger posed by employee drug use? Do you agree that there are important limits to the "prevention of harm" argument for drug testing?
6. Assuming that drug testing is justified in the particular circumstances, what procedural restrictions, if any, should be placed on it, and why?
7. Are DesJardins and Duska correct to maintain that the illegality of drug use is irrelevant?
8. How voluntary do you think employee consent to drug testing really is? Is the voluntariness of consent an important moral issue?
9. What steps do you think employers should take to deal the problem of employee drug use?

SUGGESTIONS FOR FURTHER READING

Two good, recent essays—one defending drug testing, the other arguing against it—are Michael Cranford, "Drug Testing and the Right to Privacy: Arguing the Ethics of Workplace Drug Testing," *Journal of Business Ethics* 17 (November 1998), and John R. Rowan, "Limitations on the Moral Permissibility of Employee Drug Testing," *Business and*

Professional Ethics Journal 19 (Summer 2000). Also useful are Douglas Birsch, "The Universal Drug Testing of Employees," *Business and Professional Ethics Journal* 14 (Fall 1995), and Nicholas J. Caste, "Drug Testing and Productivity," *Journal of Business Ethics* 11 (April 1992).

CHAPTER EIGHT

The Ethics of Sales

Thomas L. Carson

What are the moral obligations of salespeople? After explaining and criticizing one important answer to this question (that of David Holley), Thomas L. Carson, professor of philosophy at Loyola University of Chicago, advances his own theory, which identifies four moral duties of salespersons. Carson contends that his theory provides intuitively plausible results in concrete cases, that it avoids the weaknesses of Holley's approach, and that it explains why different kinds of salespersons have different kinds of duties to their customers. He goes on to argue that the most plausible version of the golden rule supports his theory. He concludes by discussing several examples that illustrate and clarify his theory.

THINGS TO CONSIDER

1. What's the difference between lying and deception? According to Carson, does withholding information constitute deception? What about concealing information?
2. What is the principle of *caveat emptor?* What is *merchantability?*
3. Holley writes that salespersons are required to avoid undermining the conditions of an acceptable exchange. What does he mean by an "acceptable exchange"?
4. What three criticisms of Holley does Carson make?
5 According to Carson, what four duties do salespersons have? Explain how the golden rule supports these duties.

SALES

The ethics of sales is an important, but neglected, topic in business ethics. Approximately 10 percent of the U.S. work force is involved in sales. In addition, most of us occasionally sell major holdings such as used cars and real estate. Because sales were long governed by the principle of *caveat emptor,* discussions of the ethics of sales usually focus on the ethics of withholding information and the question "What sort of information is a salesperson obligated to reveal to customers?" One of the best treatments of this topic is David Holley's paper "A Moral Evaluation of Sales Practices." In this paper, I explain Holley's theory, propose several criticisms, and formulate what I take to be a more plausible theory about the duties of salespeople. My theory avoids the objections I raise against Holley and yields intuitively plausible results when applied to cases. I also defend my theory by appeal to the golden rule and offer a defense of the version of the golden rule to which I appeal.

PRELIMINARIES: A CONCEPTUAL ROADMAP

We need to distinguish between lying, deception, withholding information, and concealing information. Roughly, deception is intentionally causing someone to have false beliefs. Standard dictionary definitions of lying say that a lie is a false statement intended to deceive others. The *Oxford English Dictionary* (1989) defines a lie as: "a false statement made with the intent to deceive." *Webster's* (1963) gives the following definition of the verb *lie:* "to make an untrue statement with intent to deceive." (We might want to add a third condition to this definition and say that in order for a false statement to be a lie, the person who makes it must know or believe that it is false. The third condition makes a difference in cases in which someone attempts to deceive another person by means of a false statement that he mistakenly believes to be true. Nothing in the present paper turns on this issue.) Lying arguably requires the intent to deceive others–I express my doubts about this in Carson (1988)–but lies that don't succeed in causing others to have false beliefs are not instances of deception. The word *deception* implies success in causing others to have false beliefs, but lying is often unsuccessful in causing deception. A further difference between lying and deception is that, while a lie must be a false statement, deception needn't involve false statements; true statements can be deceptive and many forms of deception do not involve making statements of any sort. Thus, many instances of deception do not constitute lying. Withholding information does not constitute deception. It is not a case of *causing* someone to have false beliefs; it is merely a case of failing to correct false beliefs or incomplete information. On the other hand, actively concealing information usually constitutes deception.

THE COMMON LAW PRINCIPLE OF CAVEAT EMPTOR

According to the common law principle of *caveat emptor,* sellers are not required to inform prospective buyers about the properties of the goods they sell. Under *caveat emptor,* sales and contracts to sell are legally enforceable even if the seller fails to inform the buyer of serious defects in the goods that are sold. Buyers themselves are responsible for determining the quality of the goods they purchase. In addition, English common law sometimes called for the enforcement of sales in cases in which sellers made false or misleading statements about the goods they sold (Atiyah 464–65).

Currently, all U.S. states operate under the Uniform Commercial Code of 1968. Section 2-313 of the code defines the notion of sellers' warranties (Preston 52). The code provides that all factual affirmations or statements about the goods being sold are warranties. This means that sales are not valid or legally enforceable if the seller makes false statements about the goods s/he is selling. The American legal system has developed the concept of an "implied" (as opposed to an express or explicit) warranty. Implied warranties are a significant limitation on the principle of *caveat emptor.* According to the Uniform Commercial Code, any transaction carries with it the following implied warranties: 1) that the seller owns the goods he is selling and 2) that the goods are "merchantable," i.e., suitable for the purposes for which they are sold (Preston 56–57). Many local ordinances require that people who sell real estate inform buyers about all known serious defects of the property they sell. These ordinances are also a significant limitation on the traditional principle of *caveat emptor.*

Deceptive sales practices also fall under the purview of the Federal Trade Commission (FTC). The FTC prohibits deceptive sales practices–practices likely to materially mislead reasonable consumers (FTC Statement 1983).

Many salespeople take complying with the law to be an acceptable moral standard for their conduct and claim that they have no moral duty to provide buyers with information about the goods they sell, except for that information which the law requires for an enforceable sale.

HOLLEY'S THEORY

Holley's theory is based on his concept of a "voluntary" or "mutually beneficial" market exchange (Holley uses the terms *voluntary exchange* and *mutually beneficial exchange* interchangeably). He says that a voluntary exchange occurs "only if" the following conditions are met (Holley takes his conditions to be *necessary* conditions for an acceptable exchange):

1. Both buyer and seller understand what they are giving up and what they are receiving in return.
2. Neither buyer nor seller is compelled to enter into the exchange as a result of coercion, severely restricted alternatives, or other constraints on the ability to choose.
3. Both buyer and seller are able at the time of the exchange to make rational judgments about its costs and benefits. (Holley 463)

These three conditions admit of degrees of satisfaction. An ideal exchange is an exchange involving people who are fully informed, fully rational, and "enter into the exchange entirely of their own volition" (Holley 464). The conditions for an ideal exchange are seldom, if ever, met in practice. However, Holley claims that it is still possible to have an "acceptable exchange" if the parties are "adequately informed, rational, and free from compulsion."

According to Holley, "the primary duty of salespeople to customers is to avoid undermining the conditions of an acceptable exchange." He makes it clear that, on his view, acts of omission (as well as acts of commission) can undermine the conditions of an acceptable exchange (Holley 464).

Because of the complexity of many goods and services, customers often lack information necessary for an acceptable exchange. Careful examination of products will not necessarily reveal problems or defects. According to Holley, *caveat emptor* is not acceptable as a moral principle, because customers often lack information necessary for an acceptable exchange. In such cases, salespeople are morally obligated to give information to the buyer. The question then is: *What kind of information* do salespeople need to provide buyers in order to ensure that the buyer is adequately informed? Holley attempts to answer this question in the following passage in which he appeals to the golden rule:

> Determining exactly how much information needs to be provided is not always clear-cut. We must in general rely on our assessments of what a reasonable person would want to know. As a practical guide, a salesperson might consider, "What would I want to know, if I were considering buying this product?" (Holley 467)

This principle is very demanding, perhaps more demanding than Holley realizes. Presumably, most reasonable people would *want* to know *a great deal* about the things they are thinking of buying. They might want to know *everything* relevant to the decision whether or not to buy something (more on this point shortly).

CRITICISMS OF HOLLEY

First, when time does not permit it, a salesperson cannot be morally obligated to provide all information necessary to ensure that the customer is adequately informed (all the information that a reasonable person would *want* to know if she were in the buyer's position). In many cases, reasonable customers would *want* to know a great deal of information. Often salespeople simply don't have the time to give all customers all the information Holley deems necessary for an acceptable exchange. Salespeople don't always know all the information that the buyer needs for an acceptable exchange. It cannot be a person's duty to do what is impossible—the statement that someone *ought* to do a certain act implies that she *can* do that act. Further, in many cases, salespeople don't know enough about the buyer's state of knowledge to know what information the buyer needs in order to be adequately informed. A salesperson might know that the buyer needs certain information in order to be adequately informed but not know whether or not the buyer possesses that information. One might reply that salespeople *should* know all the information necessary for an adequate exchange. However, on examination, this is not a plausible view. A salesperson in a large retail store cannot be expected to be knowledgeable about every product he sells. Often, it is impossible for realtors and used car salesmen to know much about the condition of the houses and cars they sell or the likelihood that they will need expensive repairs.

Second, Holley's theory implies that a salesperson in a store would be obligated to inform customers that a particular piece of merchandise in her store sells for less at a competing store if she knows this to be the case. (Presumably, she would *want* to know where she can get it for the lowest price, were she herself considering buying the product.) Not only do salespeople have no duty to provide this kind of information, (ordinarily) it would be wrong for them to do so.

Third, Holley's theory seems to yield unacceptable consequences in cases in which the buyer's alternatives are severely constrained. Suppose that a person with a very modest income attempts to buy a house in a small town. Her options are severely constrained, since there is only one house for sale in her price range. According to Holley, there can't be an acceptable exchange in such cases, because condition number 2 is not satisfied. However, it's not clear what he thinks sellers ought to do in such cases. The seller can't be expected to remove these constraints by giving the buyer money or building more homes in town. Holley's view seems to imply that it would be wrong for anyone to sell or rent housing to such a person. This result is unacceptable.

TOWARD A MORE PLAUSIBLE THEORY ABOUT THE ETHICS OF SALES

I believe that salespeople have the following moral duties regarding the disclosure of information when dealing with *rational adult consumers* (cases involving children or adults who are not fully rational raise special problems that I will not try to deal with here):

1. Salespeople should provide buyers with safety warnings and precautions about the goods they sell. (Sometimes it is enough for salespeople to call attention to written warnings and precautions that come with the goods and services in question. These warnings are unnecessary if the buyers already understand the dangers or precautions in question.)

2. Salespeople should refrain from lying and deception in their dealings with customers.

3. As much as their knowledge and time constraints permit, salespeople should fully answer questions about the products and services they sell. They should answer questions forthrightly and not evade questions or withhold information that has been asked for (even if this makes it less likely that they will make a successful sale). Salespeople are obligated to answer questions about the goods and services they sell. However, they are justified in refusing to answer questions that would require them to reveal information about what their competitors are selling. They are not obligated to answer questions about competing goods and services or give information about other sellers.

4. Salespeople should not try to "steer" customers toward purchases that they have reason to think will prove to be harmful to customers (financial harm counts) or that customers will come to regret.

These are prima facie duties that can conflict with other duties and are sometimes overridden by other duties. A prima facie duty is one's actual duty, other things being equal; it is an actual duty in the absence of conflicting duties of greater or equal importance. For example, my prima facie duty to keep promises is my actual duty in the absence of conflicting duties of equal or greater importance. The above is a *minimal list* of the duties of salespeople concerning the disclosure of information. I believe that the following are also prima facie duties of salespeople, but I am much less certain that these principles can be justified:

5. Salespeople should not sell customers goods or services they have reason to think will prove to be harmful to customers or that the customers will come to regret later, without giving the customers their reasons for thinking that this is the case. (This duty does not hold if the seller has good reasons to think that the customer already possesses the information in question.)

6. Salespeople should not sell items they know to be defective or of poor quality without alerting customers to this. (This duty does not hold if the buyer can be reasonably expected to know about the poor quality of what he is buying.)

I have what I take to be strong arguments for 1–4, but I'm not so sure that I can justify 5 and 6. I believe that reasonable people can disagree about 5 and 6. (I have very little to say about 5 and 6 in the present paper. See Carson [2001] for a discussion of arguments for 5 and 6.)

There are some important connections between duties 2, 4, and 6. Lying and deception in sales are not confined to lying to or deceiving customers about the goods one sells. Many salespeople misrepresent their own motives to customers/clients. Almost all salespeople invite the trust of customers/clients and claim, implicitly or explicitly, to be acting in the interests of customers/clients. Salespeople often ask customers to defer to their judgment about what is best for them. For most salespeople, gaining the trust of customers or clients is essential for success. Many salespeople are *not* interested in helping customers in the way they represent themselves as being. A salesperson who misrepresents her motives and intentions to customers violates rule 2. This simultaneous inviting and betrayal of trust is a kind of treachery. In ordinary cases, rules against lying and deception alone prohibit salespeople from steering customers toward goods or services they have reason to think will be bad for them. It is difficult to steer someone in this way without lying or deception, e.g., saying that you believe that a certain product is best for someone when you don't believe this to be the case. Similar remarks apply to selling defective goods. Often, it is impossible to do this without lying to or deceiving customers. In practice, most or many violations of rules 4 and 6 are also violations of rule 2.

A JUSTIFICATION FOR MY THEORY

Rules 1–4 yield intuitively plausible results in concrete cases and avoid all of the objections I raised against Holley. They can also be justified by appeal to the golden rule.

Taken together, rules 1–4 give us an intuitively plausible theory about the duties of salespeople regarding the disclosure of information; they give more acceptable results in actual cases than Holley's theory. They can account for cases in which the conduct of salespeople seems clearly wrong, e.g., cases of lying, deception, and steering customers into harmful decisions. Unlike Holley's theory, rules 1–4 do not make unreasonable demands on salespeople. They don't require that salespeople provide information that they don't have or spend more time with customers than they can spend. Nor do they require salespeople to divulge information about the virtues of what their competitors are selling.

In addition, my theory explains why different kinds of salespeople have different kinds of duties to their customers. For example, ordinarily, realtors have a duty to provide much more information to customers than sales clerks who sell inexpensive items in gift stores. My theory explains this difference in terms of the following:

1. the realtor's greater knowledge and expertise;
2. the much greater amount of time the realtor can devote to the customer;
3. the greater importance of the purchase of a home than the purchase of a small gift and the greater potential for harm or benefit to the buyer; and (in some cases)
4. implicit or explicit claims by the realtor to be acting on behalf of prospective home buyers (clerks in stores rarely make such claims).

The Golden Rule

I think that the golden rule is most plausibly construed as a consistency principle (those who violate the golden rule are guilty of inconsistency). The following version of the golden rule can be justified:

> GR. Consistency requires that if you think that it would be morally permissible for someone to do a certain act to another person, then you must consent to someone else doing the same act to you in relevantly similar circumstances.

How the Golden Rule Supports My Theory

Given this version of the golden rule, any rational and consistent moral judge who makes judgments about the moral obligations of salespeople will have to accept rules 1–4 as prima facie duties. Consider each duty in turn:

1. All of us have reason to fear the hazards about us in the world; we depend on others to warn us of those hazards. Few people would survive to adulthood were it not for the warnings of others about such things as oncoming cars, live electric wires, and approaching tor-

nadoes. No one who values her own life can honestly say that she is willing to have others fail to warn her of dangers.

2. Like everyone else, a salesperson needs correct information in order to act effectively to achieve her goals and advance her interests. She is not willing to act on the basis of false beliefs. Consequently, she is not willing to have others deceive her or lie to her about matters relevant to her decisions in the marketplace. She is not willing to have members of other professions (such as law and medicine) make it a policy to deceive her or lie to her whenever they can gain financially from doing so.

3. Salespeople have questions about the goods and services they themselves buy. They can't say that they are willing to have others evade or refuse to answer those questions. We want our questions to be answered by salespeople or else we wouldn't ask them. We are not willing to have salespeople evade or refrain from answering our questions. (Digression. Rule 3 permits salespeople to refuse to answer questions that would force them to provide information about their competitors. Why should we say *this?* Why not say instead that salespeople are obligated to answer *all questions* that customers ask? The answer is as follows: A salesperson's actions affect *both* her customers and her employer. In applying the golden rule to this issue she can't simply ask what kind of information she would want were she in the customer's position [Holley poses the question in just this way]. Rule 3 can probably be improved upon, but it is a decent first approximation. A disinterested person who was not trying to give preference to the interests of salespeople, employers, or customers could endorse 3 as a policy for salespeople to follow. We can and must recognize the legitimacy of employers' demands for loyalty. The role of being an advocate or agent for someone who is selling things is legitimate within certain bounds—almost all of us are willing to have real estate agents work for us. A rational person could consent to the idea that everyone follow principles such as rule 3.)

4. All of us are capable of being manipulated by others into doing things that harm us, especially in cases in which others are more knowledgeable than we are. No one can consent to the idea that other people (or salespeople) should manipulate us into doing things that harm us whenever doing so is to their own advantage. Salespeople who claim that it would be permissible for them to make it a policy to deceive customers, fail to warn them about dangers, evade their questions, or manipulate them into doing things that are harmful to them whenever doing so is advantageous to them are inconsistent because they are not willing to have others do the same to them. They must allow that 1–4 are prima facie moral duties.

Rules 1–4 are only prima facie duties. The golden rule can account for the cases in which 1–4 are overridden by other more important duties. For example, we would be willing to have other people violate rules 1–4 if doing so were necessary in order to save the life of an innocent person. In practice, violating 1, 2, 3, or 4 is permissible only in very rare cases. The financial interests of salespeople seldom justify violations of 1, 2, 3, or 4. The fact that a salesperson can make more money by violating 1, 2, 3, or 4 would not justify her in violating any of these unless she has very pressing financial obligations that she cannot meet otherwise. Often, salespeople need to meet certain minimum sales quotas to avoid being fired. Suppose that a salesperson needs to make it a policy to violate 1–4 in order to meet her sales quotas and keep her job. Would this justify her in violating 1–4? *Possibly.* But, in order for this to be the case, the following conditions would have to be met: a) she has important moral obligations such as feeding and housing her family that require her to be employed (needing money to keep one's family in an expensive house or take them to Disney World wouldn't justify violating 1–4); and b) she can't find another job that would enable her to meet her obligations without violating 1–4 (or other equally important duties). Those salespeople who can't keep their jobs or make an adequate income without violating 1–4 should seek other lines of employment.

A Defense of the Version of the Golden Rule Employed Earlier

My argument is as follows:

1. Consistency requires that if you think that it would be morally permissible for someone to do a certain act to another person, then you must grant that it would be morally permissible for someone to do that same act to you in relevantly similar circumstances.

2. Consistency requires that if you think that it would be morally permissible for someone to do a certain act to you in certain circumstances, then you must *consent* to him/her doing that act to you in those circumstances.

Therefore,

> GR. Consistency requires that if you think that it would be morally permissible for someone to do a certain act to another person, then you must consent to (not object to) someone doing the same act to you in relevantly similar circumstances. (You are inconsistent if you think that it would be morally permissible for someone to do a certain act to another person, but do not consent to someone doing the same act to you in relevantly similar circumstances.) (This argument follows the argument given by Gensler 89–90).

This argument is valid, i.e., the conclusion follows from the premises, and both its premises are true. Both premises are consistency requirements. Premise 1 addresses questions about the consistency of a person's different moral beliefs. Premise 2 addresses questions about whether a person's moral beliefs are consistent with her attitudes and actions. Our attitudes and actions can be either consistent or inconsistent with the moral judgments we accept.

Premise 1

Premise 1 follows from, or is a narrower version of, the universalizability principle (UP). The UP can be stated as follows:

> Consistency requires that, if one makes a moral judgment about a particular case, then one must make the same moral judgment about any similar case, unless there is a morally relevant difference between the cases.

Premise 1 is a principle of consistency for judgments about the moral permissibility of actions. The UP, by contrast, is a principle of consistency for *any kind of moral judgment,* including judgments about what things are good and bad.

Premise 2

How shall we understand what is meant by "consenting to" something? For our present purposes, we should not take consenting to something to be the same as desiring it or trying to bring it about. My thinking that it is morally permissible for you to beat me at chess does not commit me to desiring that you beat me, nor does it commit me to playing so as to allow you to beat me. Consenting to an action is more like not objecting to it, not criticizing, or not resenting, the other person for doing it. If I think that it is permissible for you to beat me at chess then I cannot object to your beating me. I am inconsistent if I object to your doing something that I take to be morally permissible. If I claim that it is permissible for someone to do something to another person, then, on pain of inconsistency, I cannot object if someone else does the same thing to me in relevantly similar circumstances. The gist of my application of the golden rule to sales is that since we *do object* to salespeople doing such things as lying to us, deceiving us, and failing to answer our questions, we cannot consistently say that it is morally permissible for them to *do* these things.

EXAMPLES

I will discuss several cases to illustrate and clarify my theory.

Example A

I am selling a used car that I know has bad brakes; this is one of the reasons I am selling the car. You don't ask me any questions about the car, and I sell it to you without informing you of the problem with the brakes.

Example B

I am selling a used car that starts poorly in cold weather. You arrange to look at the car early in the morning on a very cold day. I don't own a garage so the car is out in the cold. With difficulty, I start it up and drive it for thirty minutes shortly before you look at it and then cover the car with snow to make it seem as if it hasn't been driven. The engine is still hot when you come and the car starts up immediately. You then purchase the car, remarking that you need a car that starts well in the cold to get to work, since you don't have a garage.

Example C

While working as a salesperson, I feign a friendly concern for a customer's interests. I say, "I will try to help you find the product that is best suited for your needs. I don't want you to spend any more money than you need to. Take as much time as you need." The customer believes me, but she is deceived. In fact, I couldn't care less about her welfare. I only want to sell her the highest priced item I can as quickly as I can. I don't like the customer, indeed, I am contemptuous of her.

In example A, I violate rule 1 and put the buyer and other motorists, passengers, and pedestrians at risk. In example B, I violate rules 2 and 5. In example C, I violate rule 2. In the absence of conflicting obligations that are at least as important as the rules I violate, my actions in cases A-C are morally wrong.

Example D: A Longer Case (an actual case)

In 1980, I received a one-year fellowship from The National Endowment for the Humanities. The fellowship paid for my salary, but not my fringe benefits. Someone in the benefits office of my university told me that I had the option of continuing my health insurance through the university if I paid for the premiums out of my own pocket. I told the benefits person that this was a lousy deal and that I could do better by going to a private insurance company. I went to the office of Prudential Insurance agent Mr. A. O. "Ed" Mokarem. I told him that I was looking for a one-year medical insurance policy to cover me during the period of the fellowship and that I planned to resume my university policy when I returned to teaching. (The university provided this policy free of charge to all faculty who were teaching.) He showed me a comparable Prudential policy that cost about half as much as the university's policy. He explained the policy to me. I asked him to fill out the forms so that I could purchase the policy. He then told me that there was a potential problem I should consider. He said roughly the following:

> You will want to return to your free university policy next year when you return to teaching. The Prudential policy is a one-year terminal policy. If you develop any serious medical problems during the next year, Prudential will probably consider you "uninsurable" and will not be willing to sell you health insurance in the future. If you buy the Prudential policy, you may encounter the same problems with your university policy. Since you will be dropping this policy *voluntarily,* they will have the right to underwrite your application for re-enrollment. If you develop a serious health problem during the next year, their underwriting decision could be "Total Rejection," imposing

some waivers and/or exclusions, or (at best) subjecting your coverage to the "pre-existing conditions clause," which would not cover any pre-existing conditions until you have been covered under the new policy for at least a year.

If I left my current health insurance for a year, I risked developing a costly medical condition for which no one would be willing to insure me. That would have been a very foolish risk to take. So, I thanked him very much and, swallowing my pride, went back to renew my health insurance coverage through the university. I never bought any insurance from Mr. Mokarem and never had occasion to send him any business.

I have discussed this case with numerous classes through the years. It usually generates a lively discussion. Most of my students do not think that Mr. Mokarem was morally obligated to do what he did, but they don't think that what he did was wrong either—they regard his actions as supererogatory or above and beyond the call of duty.

My view about example D

On my theory, this is a difficult case to assess. If rules 1–4 are a salesperson's only duties concerning the disclosure of information, then Mr. Mokarem was not obligated to inform me as he did. (In this case, the information in question was information about a *competing product*—the university's health insurance policy.) If rule 5 is a prima facie duty of salespeople, then (assuming that he had no conflicting moral duties of greater or equal importance) it was his duty, all things considered, to inform me as he did. Since I am uncertain that 5 can be justified, I'm not sure whether or not Mr. Mokarem was obligated to do what he did or whether his actions were supererogatory. This case illustrates part of what is at stake in the question of whether rule 5 is a prima facie duty of salespeople.

Acknowledgments—This essay is a revised and abridged version of material from two earlier essays, "Deception and Withholding Information in Sales," *Business Ethics Quarterly* 11 (2001): 275–306, and "Ethical Issues in Selling and Advertising," *The Blackwell Guide to Business Ethics*, ed. Norman Bowie (Oxford: Blackwell, 2002), 186–205. Many thanks to Ivan Preston for his very generous and helpful advice and criticisms. Everyone interested in these topics should read his work.

REFERENCES

Atiyah, P. S. (1979) *The Rise and Fall of Freedom of Contract*. Oxford: The Clarendon Press.

Carson, Thomas. (1988) "On the definition of lying: a reply to Jones and revisions." *Journal of Business Ethics*, 7: 509–14.

Carson, Thomas. (2001) "Deception and withholding information in sales." *Business Ethics Quarterly* 11: 275–306.

FTC policy statement on deception. (1983–still current) Available on the Web at: http.://www.ftc.gov/bcp/guides/guides.htm then click on FTC Policy Statement on Deception.

Gensler, Harry. (1986) "A Kantian argument against abortion." *Philosophical Studies* 49: 83–98.

Holley, David. (1993) "A moral evaluation of sales practices." In Tom Beauchamp and Norman Bowie, eds., *Ethical Theory and Business*, fourth edition, 462–72. Englewood Cliffs, NJ: Prentice Hall.

Preston, Ivan. (1975) *The Great American Blow-up: Puffery in Advertising and Selling*. Madison: University of Wisconsin Press, 1975.

REVIEW AND DISCUSSION QUESTIONS

1. Have you encountered unethical conduct by a salesperson? Is such conduct widespread, or do most salespersons try to behave ethically? When salespersons do act unethically, what explains this, and what can be done about it?
2. Critically assess Carson's criticisms of Holley's theory. Do you find them persuasive?
3. Do Carson's rules 1 through 4 provide a more plausible account of the ethics of sales than Holley's theory does? Explain why or why not. Do you agree that the actions in examples A, B, and C are morally wrong?
4. Is Carson's interpretation of the golden rule the best way of understanding it? In your view, is the golden rule a basic principle of ethics? Explain why or why not. What implications does the golden rule have for salespeople?
5. Carson believes that he makes a strong case for rules 1 through 4, but that reasonable people can disagree about rules 5 and 6. In your view, do salespersons have a duty to follow rules 5 and 6? In example D, was Mr. Mokarem morally obligated to do what he did?
6. Do salespeople ever face ethical issues that Carson's theory doesn't answer? If so, give an example.

SUGGESTIONS FOR FURTHER READING

David M. Holley's essay, "A Moral Evaluation of Sales Practices," originally appeared in *Business and Professional Ethics Journal* 5 (Fall 1987). Holley revisits the issue in "Information Disclosure in Sales," *Journal of Business Ethics* 17 (April 1998), and replies to Carson in "Alternative Approaches to Applied Ethics: A Response to Carson's Critique," *Business Ethics Quarterly* 12 (January 2002). For further discussion of the ethics of sales, see James M. Ebejer and Michael J. Morden, "Paternalism in the Marketplace: Should a Salesman Be His Buyer's Keeper?" *Journal of Business Ethics* 7 (May 1988), Kerry S. Walters, "Limited Paternalism and the Pontius Pilate Plight," *Journal of Business Ethics* 8 (December 1989), and George Brockway, "Limited Paternalism and the Salesperson: A Reconsideration," *Journal of Business Ethics* 12 (April 1993).

CHAPTER NINE

◆

The Inconclusive Ethical Case
Against Manipulative Advertising

Michael J. Phillips

John Kenneth Galbraith and other critics of advertising have long con-
tended that it manipulates our needs and fears, increasing our propensity to consume and swaying our individual purchasing decisions.
Granting for the sake of argument that the critics of advertising are correct about its effectiveness, Michael J. Phillips, professor emeritus of
business administration at Indiana University, assesses four possible attacks on manipulative advertising, each from a different ethical perspective: namely, that manipulative advertising has negative consequences for utility, that it undermines personal autonomy, that it
violates Kant's categorical imperative, and that it weakens the personal
virtue of both its practitioners and victims. After considering one final,
partial defense of manipulative advertising, he concludes that although
the practice is morally problematic, there is room for doubt about its
badness and no completely definite basis for condemning it.

THINGS TO CONSIDER

1. What is "manipulative advertising"? What is "associative advertising"?
2. Galbraith's "dependence effect" refers to the relationship between
   production and consumer wants. What exactly is the dependence
   effect?
3. Explain Theodore Levitt's statement that "the promises and images
   which imaginative ads . . . induce in us are as much the product
   as the physical materials themselves." In what way is he offering a
   defense of manipulative advertising?
4. Hare makes two Kantian arguments against manipulative advertis-

From *Business and Professional Ethics Journal* 13 (Winter 1994). Reprinted by permission of
the author. Some notes and references omitted.

ing (based on different ways of formulating Kant's categorical imperative). What are they?
5. What is manipulative advertising's "last defense"?

This article explores the ethical implications of [the] perception that advertisers successfully "exploit and manipulate the vast range of human fears and needs." It begins by defining its sense of the term *manipulative advertising*. Then the article asserts for purposes of argument that manipulative advertising actually works. Specifically, I make two controversial assumptions about such advertising: (1) that it plays a major role in increasing the general propensity to consume, and (2) that it powerfully influences individual consumer purchase decisions. With the deck thus stacked against manipulative advertising, the article goes on to inquire whether either assumption justifies its condemnation, by considering four ethical criticisms of manipulative advertising. Ethically, I conclude, manipulative advertising is a most problematic practice. If probabilistic assertions are valid in ethics, that is, the odds strongly favor the conclusion that manipulative advertising is wrong. Nevertheless, there still is room for doubt about its badness. Like the apparently easy kill that continually slips out of the hunter's sights, manipulative advertising evades the clean strike that would justify its condemnation for once and all.

WHAT IS MANIPULATIVE ADVERTISING?

. . . What, then, is manipulative advertising? . . . I define "manipulative advertising" as advertising that tries to favorably alter consumers' perceptions of the advertised product by appeals to factors other than the product's physical attributes and functional performance. There is no sharp line between such advertising and advertising that is nonmanipulative; even purely informative ads are unlikely to feature unattractive people and depressing surroundings. Nor is it clear what proportion of American advertising can fairly be classed as manipulative. Suffice it to say that that proportion almost certainly is significant. As we will see, advertising's critics sometimes seem to think that all of it is manipulative.

Perhaps the most common example of manipulative advertising is a technique John Waide (1987, 73–74) calls "associative advertising." Advertisers using this technique try to favorably influence consumer perceptions of a product by associating it with a nonmarket good (e.g., contentment, sex, vigor, power, status, friendship, or family) that the product ordinarily cannot supply on its own. By purchasing the product, their ads suggest, the consumer somehow will get the nonmarket good. Michael Schudson describes this familiar form of advertising as follows: "The ads say, typically, 'buy me and you will overcome the anxieties I have just reminded you about' or 'buy me and you will enjoy life' or 'buy me and be recognized as a successful person' or 'buy me and everything will be easier for you' or 'come spend a few dollars and share in this society of freedom, choice, novelty, and abundance'" (1986, 6). Through such linkages between product and nonmarket good, associative advertising seeks to increase the product's perceived value and thus to induce its purchase. Because these linkages (e.g., the connection between beer and attractive women) generally make little sense, such advertising is far removed from rational persuasion.

THE EFFECTS OF MANIPULATIVE ADVERTISING: WHAT THE CRITICS THINK

In the previous section, I tried to describe manipulative advertising in terms of sellers' *efforts*, rather than their actual accomplishments. But does manipulative advertising successfully influence consumers? As might be expected, advertising's critics generally answer this question in the affirmative. Perhaps the best-known example is chapter XI of John Kenneth Galbraith's *The Affluent Society*, where he described his well-known dependence effect.

Galbraith's dependence effect might be described as the way the process of consumer goods production creates and satisfies consumer wants (1958, 158). "That wants are, in fact, the fruit of production," he intoned, "will now be denied by few serious scholars" (154). In part, these wants result from emulation, as increased production means increased consumption for some, followed by even more consumption as others follow suit (154–55). But advertising and salesmanship provide an even more direct link between production and consumer wants. Those practices, Galbraith says:

> [C]annot be reconciled with the notion of independently determined desires, for their central function is to create desires. . . . This is accomplished by the producer of goods or at his behest. A broad

empirical relationship exists between what is spent on production of consumers' goods and what is spent in synthesizing the desires for that production. A new consumer product must be introduced with a suitable advertising campaign to arouse an interest in it. The path for an expansion of output must be paved by a suitable expansion in the advertising budget. Outlays for the manufacturing of a product are not more important in the strategy of modern business enterprise than outlays for the manufacturing of demand for the product. (155–56)

. . . To Galbraith, therefore, advertising in general is manipulative. In *The Affluent Society,* it apparently worked mainly to promote aggregate demand, rather than to shift demand from one brand to another. Many of advertising's critics follow Galbraith's lead by stressing how it socializes people to embrace consumerist values. . . .

From all this, it is a short step to the notion that advertising plays a major role in shaping and sustaining the modern society of material abundance. Implicitly, at least, some accounts of this kind liken society to a huge machine whose aim is the conversion of natural resources into consumer products. For the machine to work properly, its human components must be motivated to play their role in producing those products. This can be accomplished by: (1) implanting in people an intense desire for consumer goods, and (2) requiring that they do productive work to get the money to buy those goods. . . . Galbraith suggested that these social imperatives of production and consumption make the worker/consumer resemble a squirrel who races full-tilt to keep abreast of a wheel propelled by his own efforts (1958, 154, 159).

Although they naturally evaluate the matter differently, business leaders often second the argument that advertising is essential to prosperity. In . . . an exchange on advertising expenditures by the fast-food industry, William H. Genge, the chairman of Ketchum Communications' board, wrote:

> I regard the many millions of dollars spent by fast-food companies (and other retailers as well) as healthy and necessary stimulation of the consumption that makes our economy the most dynamic and productive in the world.
>
> Some people talk as though large advertising budgets are wasteful and nonproductive. It just takes one simple question to put that down. The question is: Where does the money go? The answer is: It provides jobs and livelihoods for hundreds of thousands of people–

not only in the advertising and communications sector but for all the people employed by fast-food companies and, indeed, all marketing organizations. (1985, 58–59)

"So," Genge concluded, "large advertising expenditures are not a misallocation of economic resources. They are, in fact, an essential allocation and the driving force behind consumption, job creation, and prosperity" (59).

Advertising that is sufficiently manipulative to create a consumer society also might be able to determine consumers' individual purchase decisions. Most often, I suppose, these would be brand choices within a particular product category, although advertising might also steer people toward certain products and away from others. . . .

ASSUMPTIONS AND PLAN OF ATTACK

As we have just seen, many critics of advertising say that it socializes people to a life of consumption. And some regard it as a strong influence on individual brand or product decisions. However, these beliefs are not universally shared. Some students of advertising doubt that ads do much to dictate individual brand choices. And even if advertising strongly influences consumer decisions, it does not follow that any specific ad invariably compels the purchase of the product it touts. The reason is that a particular product advertisement is only one of many factors—especially competing advertisements—influencing consumers (Hayek 1961, 347). For the same general reason, it is difficult to assess advertising's role in making people lifetime consumers. . . .

Despite such difficulties, this article assumes for the sake of argument that manipulative advertising really works. Thus, I assume that such advertising strongly influences individual purchase decisions, and that it plays a major role in producing consumerist attitudes among the populace. In neither case, however, do I wish to specify all the links in the causal chain through which manipulative advertising does its work. In particular, I make no assumptions about the personal traits that render consumers responsive to manipulative advertising. Later in the article, for example, I consider the possibility that manipulative advertising succeeds because consumers want and need it.

Operating under the assumptions just stated, I now consider four possible ethical attacks on manipulative advertising. These are the claims that such advertising: (1) has negative consequences for utility, (2) undermines personal autonomy, (3) violates Kant's categorical imperative, and (4) weakens the personal virtue of its practitioners and its victims. I also consider one qualified defense of manipulative advertising: that even though no moral person would choose it were he writing on a clean slate, by now its elimination would be worse than its continuance.[1]

For each attack on manipulative advertising, I assume the validity of the relevant moral value or ethical theory, thus precluding defenses of manipulative advertising that attack the value or theory itself. . . .

UTILITARIANISM

As just stated, this article assumes that advertising can manipulate people in two distinct ways: (1) by socializing them to embrace consumerist values, and (2) by dictating individual purchase decisions. One important utilitarian criticism of manipulative advertising seems mainly to involve the first of these effects. Another implicates the second effect. . . . I now discuss each of these utilitarian attacks in turn. Throughout, I explicitly or implicitly compare my assumed world in which manipulative advertising exists and is effective with a world in which all advertising is merely informative.

The Implications of the Dependence Effect

The Affluent Society marked Galbraith's arrival as a critic of consumer society and its works. For his critique to be persuasive, he had to counter the argument that America's enormous production of consumer goods is justified because people want, enjoy, and demand them. This required that he undermine at least two widespread beliefs: (1) that consumer desires are genuinely autonomous, and (2) that they produce significant satisfactions. As we saw earlier, he attacked the first assumption by maintaining that consumer wants are created by the productive process through which they are satisfied, with advertising serving as the main generator of those wants. This argument would have enabled Galbraith to contend that advertising is bad because it denies autonomy, but he seemed not to emphasize that point. Instead, he maintained that the satisfaction of advertising-induced desires generates little additional utility. His argument was that if advertising is needed to arouse consumer wants, they cannot be too strong. "The fact that wants can be synthesized by advertising, catalyzed by salesmanship, and shaped by the discreet manipulations of the persuaders shows that they are not very urgent. A man who is hungry need never be told of his need for food" (1958, 158).

As a result, Galbraith continued, one cannot assume that the increased production characterizing the modern affluent society generates corresponding increases in utility. Instead, as he summarizes the matter:

> [O]ur concern for goods . . . does not arise in spontaneous consumer need. Rather, the dependence effect means that it grows out of the process of production itself. If production is to increase, the wants must be effectively contrived. In the absence of the contrivance the increase would not occur. This is not true of all goods, but that it is true of a substantial part is sufficient. It means that since the demand for this part would not exist, were it not contrived, its utility or urgency, ex contrivance, is zero. If we regard this production as marginal, we may say that the marginal utility of present aggregate output, ex advertising and salesmanship, is zero. (160)

Because wants must be contrived for production to increase, on Galbraith's assumptions production would be lower were advertising completely informative. Since on those assumptions that contrived production generates little additional utility, however, the loss would not be much felt. Indeed, with resources shifted away from advertising and consumption and toward activities that improve the quality of our lives, overall utility might well grow in manipulative advertising's absence.

Galbraith's basic argument was that because consumer wants are contrived, they are not urgent; and that because they are not urgent, their satisfaction does not generate much utility. One way to attack his argument is to maintain that consumer desires really do arise from within the individual, but my two assumptions foreclose that possibility here. Another is to follow the lead established by Friedrich Hayek's 1961 critique of Galbraith's dependence effect. To Hayek, Galbraith's argument involves a massive non sequitur: the attempt to reason from a desire's origin outside the individual to its unimportance (1961, 346–47). If that assertion were valid, he thought, it would follow that "the whole cultural achievement of man is not important" (346).

> Surely an individual's want for literature is not original with himself in the sense that he would experience it if literature were not produced. Does this mean that the production of literature cannot be defended as satisfying a want because it is only the production which provokes the demand? In this, as in the case of all cultural needs, it is unquestionably, in Professor Galbraith's words, "the process of satisfying the wants that creates the wants." (347)

Presumably, the same general point applies to utility-maximization. Just because product desire A originated within Cal Consumer while product desire B came his way through manipulative advertising, it does not follow that satisfying desire A would give him more utility than satisfying desire B. Indeed, as we will see presently, the opposite may be true.

The Frustration of Rational Interbrand Choices

The second major utilitarian objection to manipulative advertising concerns its power to distort consumer choices among brands and products. As R. M. Hare once observed:

> [T]he market economy is only defensible if it really does . . . lead to the maximum satisfaction of the preferences of the public. And it will not do this if it is distorted by various well-known undesirable practices. . . . By bringing it about that people decide on their purchases . . . after being deceived or in other ways manipulated, fraudulent advertisers impair the wisdom of the choices that the public makes and so distort the market in such a way that it does not function to maximize preference-satisfactions. (Hare 1984, 27–28)

For example, now suppose that Cal Consumer's preferences would find their optimum satisfaction in Product A. Intoxicated by Product B's manipulative advertising, Cal instead buys that product, which satisfies his original preferences less well than Product A. If Cal would have bought Product A in a regime where advertising is purely informative, presumably B's manipulative advertising cost him some utility.

The previous argument, however, might fail if manipulative advertising gives consumers satisfactions that they would not otherwise obtain from their purchases. In that event, the utility lost when manipulative advertising causes consumers to choose the wrong product for their needs must be weighed against the utility consumers gain from such advertising. Due to the inherent uncertainty of utility calculations, it may be unclear which effect would predominate. Sometimes, though, the gains could outweigh the losses: that is, manipulative advertising could generate more utility than purely informative advertising.

But how can "manipulated" desires and purchases generate more utility than their "rational" counterparts? One answer emerges from the dark masterpiece of the literature on manipulative advertising—Theodore Levitt's 1970 contribution to the *Harvard Business Review*. Levitt's main thesis is that "embellishment and distortion are among advertising's legitimate and socially desirable purposes" (Levitt 1970, 85). His determinedly nonlinear argument for that conclusion may be regarded as proceeding through several steps. The first is his assertion that when seen without illusions, human life is a poor thing. Natural reality, Levitt insists, is "crudely fashioned"; "crude, drab, and generally oppressive"; and "drab, dull, [and] anguished" (86, 90). For this reason, people try to transcend it whenever they can. "Everybody everywhere wants to modify, transform, embellish, enrich, and reconstruct the world around him—to introduce into an otherwise harsh or bland existence some sort of purposeful and distorting alleviation" (87). People do so mainly though artistic endeavor, but also through advertising. "[W]e use art, architecture, literature, and the rest, and advertising as well, to shield ourselves, in advance of experience, from the stark and plain reality in which we are fated to live" (90). Thus, "[m]any of the so-called distortions of advertising, product design, and packaging may be viewed as a paradigm of the many responses that man makes to the conditions of survival in the environment" (90).

From all this, it follows that consumers demand more than "pure operating functionality" from the products they buy (89). As Charles Revson of Revlon, Inc. once said: "'In the factory we make cosmetics; in the store we sell hope'" (85). Thus, "[i]t is not cosmetic chemicals women want, but the seductive charm promised by the alluring symbols with which these chemicals have been surrounded—hence the rich and exotic packages in which they are sold, and the suggestive advertising with which they are promoted" (85). In other words, consumers demand an expanded notion of functionality which includes "'non-mechanical' utilities," and do so to "help . . . solve a problem of life" (89). Therefore, "the product" they buy includes not only narrowly functional attributes, but also the emotional or affective content produced by its packaging and advertising. "The promises and images which imaginative ads and sculptured packages induce in us are as much the product as the physical materials themselves. . . . [T]hese ads and packagings describe the product's fullness for us; in our minds, the product becomes a complex abstraction which is . . . the conception of a perfection which has not yet been experienced" (89–90). . . .

To Levitt, therefore, we do not merely buy a physical product, but also a set of positive feelings connected with it by advertising. If his argument is sound, those feelings give us extra utility above and beyond the utility we get from the product's performance of its functions. This extra utility might well outweigh the utility we lose because manipulative advertising has made us buy a product that is suboptimum in purely functional terms and that we would not have bought were advertising only informative.

Is Levitt's argument sound? Although his description may not apply to all people, or even to most, it hardly seems ridiculous. People who object to Levitt's contention that human life is crude, drab, and dull should recall that he is speaking of a human life we infrequently experience—human life absent the embellishments all civilizations try to give it. If his contention is correct, the need to transcend our natural condition is an obvious motive for those embellishments. John Waide, however, insists that our need for embellishment can be satisfied without manipulative advertising—through, for example, ideals, fantasies, heroes, and dreams (Waide 1987, 76). But why assume this? If the need for comforting illusions is strong and pervasive, why should embellishment not extend to the products people buy?

Bigger problems, however, arise from Levitt's assumption that consumers are aware of advertising's illusions. If people know that advertising lies, how can they derive much psychic benefit—i.e., much utility—from its embellishments? Worse yet, products tend not to deliver on manipulative advertising's promises of sex, status, security, and the like. When this is so, how can such advertising deliver much utility to the consumers it controls (cf. Waide 1987, 75)? Indeed, the gap between manipulative advertising's implicit promises and its actual performance may lead to frustrated expectations and significant *dis*utility.

Recall, however, that for Levitt consumers want and need to be manipulated because life without advertising's illusions is too much to bear. If so, it is unlikely that everyone would be *continuously* aware of advertising's illusions and the low chance of their realization. Only intermittently, in other words, would people assume a tough-minded, rational-actor mentality toward advertising. On other occasions, some would effectively suspend disbelief in advertising's embellishments. Although they might retain latent knowledge of those illusions, that knowledge would not be constantly present to their consciousness. And when the illusions rule, they could generate real satisfactions.

Are these assumptions about consumers realistic ones? To me, they are plausible as applied to some people some of the time. . . . There . . . is nothing ridiculous in assuming that people gain utility by accepting advertising's illusions, while retaining some latent and/or intermittent knowledge of their condition. . . .

AUTONOMY

All things considered, the utilitarian arguments against manipulative advertising are unimpressive. Indeed, utilitarianism might even support that practice. Galbraith claimed that little utility is generated when we satisfy contrived wants. But the connection between a desire's origin outside the individual and the low utility resulting from its satisfaction is unclear. At first glance, it appears that manipulative advertising robs consumers of utility by inducing them to buy functionally suboptimal products. But while this may be true, the resulting utility losses arguably are counterbalanced by the utility people gain from manipulative advertising. . . .

The Autonomy-Related Objection to Manipulative Advertising

To some people, however, the preceding points may say more about utilitarianism's deficiencies than about manipulative advertising's worth. One standard criticism of utilitarianism emphasizes its indifference to the moral quality of the means by which utility is maximized. Thus, even if manipulative advertising increases consumers' utility, it is bad because it does so by suppressing their ability to make intelligent, self-directed product choices on the basis of their own values and interests. In a word, manipulative advertising now seems objectionable because it denies personal *autonomy*.

Among the many strands within the notion of autonomy, one of the most common equates it with self-government or self-determination. According to Steven Lukes, for example, autonomy is "self-direction"; the autonomous person's "thought and action is his own, and [is] not determined by agencies or causes outside his control" (Lukes 1973, 52). At the social level, Lukes adds, an individual is autonomous "to the degree to which he subjects the pressures and norms with which he is confronted to conscious and critical evaluation, and forms intentions and reaches practical decisions as the result of independent and rational reflection" (52).

If manipulative advertising has the effects this article assumes, it apparently denies autonomy to the individuals it successfully controls. On this article's assumptions, people become consumers and make product choices precisely through "agencies and causes outside [their] control," and not through "conscious and critical evaluation" or "independent and rational reflection." To Lippke, moreover, advertising also has an "implicit content" that further suppresses autonomy. Among other things, this implicit content causes people to accept emotionalized, superficial, and oversimplified claims; desire ease and gratification rather than austerity and self-restraint; let advertisers dictate the meaning of the good life; defer to their peers; and think that consumer products are a means for acquiring life's nonmaterial goods (44–47). People so constituted are unlikely to be independent, self-governing agents who subject all social pressures to an internal critique. Nor is it likely that they would have much resistance to manipulative appeals to buy particular products.

Are Consumers Autonomous on Levitt's Assumptions?

On Levitt's assumptions, however, perhaps consumers do act autonomously when they submit to manipulative advertising. If Levitt is correct: (1) manipulative advertising works much as its critics say that it works; because (2) consumers suspend disbelief in its claims and embrace its illusions; because (3) they want, need, and demand those illusions to cope with human existence; while (4) nonetheless knowing on some level that those illusions indeed are illusions. In sum, one might say, advertising manipulates consumers because they knowingly and rationally want to be manipulated. That is, they half-consciously sacrifice their autonomy for reasons that make some sense on Levitt's assumptions about human life. In still other words, they more or less autonomously relinquish their autonomy. . . .

Levitt's argument, however, appears to concern only individual purchase decisions, and not advertising's assumed ability to socialize people to accept consumerism and reject autonomy. But his argument is broad enough to explain this second process. On Levitt's assumptions, people would more or less knowingly embrace consumerism because unfiltered reality is too much to bear, and would reject autonomy in favor of Lippke's "implicit content" because autonomy offers too little payoff at too much cost. If those assumptions are accurate, moreover, people arguably have sound reasons for behaving in these ways. . . .

THE CATEGORICAL IMPERATIVE

One problem with some of the claims discussed thus far is that they present difficult empirical issues. This is plainly true of Levitt's claims. It also is true of Galbraith's assertion that because advertising-induced wants originate outside the individual, they have low urgency and therefore generate little utility when they are satisfied. The same can be said of Hayek's response to Galbraith. Given these problems, maybe manipulative advertising is best addressed by ethical theories whose conclusions do not depend on empirical matters such as consumer psychology, or on manipulation's consequences for utility. Kant's categorical imperative is an obvious candidate.

R. M. Hare made two Kantian arguments against manipulative advertising. "Kantians will say . . . that to manipulate people is not to treat them as ends—certainly not as autonomous legislating members of a kingdom of ends. . . . But even apart from that it is something that we prefer not to happen to us and therefore shall not will it as a universal maxim" (Hare 1984, 28). His reference, of course, was to the two major formulations of Kant's categorical imperative. The first, which comes in several versions, underlies Hare's second argument. The version employed here goes as follows: "Act only on that maxim through which you can at the same time will that it should become a universal law" (Kant 1964, 88). According to the second major formulation of the imperative, one must "[a]ct in such a way that you always treat humanity, whether in your own person or in the person of any other, never simply as a means, but always at the same time as an end" (96).

Under either formulation of the imperative, it seems, manipulative advertising stands condemned. Under the first formulation, it seems difficult to identify a maxim that would: (1) clearly justify manipulative advertising, and (2) be universalized by any advertiser. Consider, for example, the following possibility: "In order to induce purchases and make money, business people can use advertising tactics that undermine the rational evaluation and choice of products by associating them with desired states to which they have little or no real relation." Presumably, no one would will the maxim's universalization, because to do so is to waive any moral objection to manipulative advertising aimed at oneself. Manipulative advertising apparently fares even worse under the second statement of the categorical imperative. As James Rachels has noted, under this formulation "we may never *manipulate* people, or *use* people, to achieve our purposes" (Rachels 1993, 129). Instead, we should respect their rational nature by giving them the information that will enable them to make informed, autonomous decisions (Rachels 1993, 129–30). As the term *manipulative advertising* suggests, businesses that employ it to generate sales obviously try to use people as means to their own ends, and do so precisely by undermining their rationality and their ability to make informed, autonomous decisions.

Even in the Kantian realm, however, empirical concerns intrude. Suppose again that Levitt is right in claiming that people want and need manipulative advertising. Given this assumption, the relevant maxim becomes something like the following: "In order to induce purchases and make money, people can use manipulative advertising tactics that undermine the rational evaluation and choice of products and services, but only when such advertising tactics liberate consumers from their dark, stark, and depressing natural existence." Although I cannot speak for everyone (or for Kant), I might will this maxim's universalization if I found Levitt's conception of the human condition at all plausible. This illustrates a common criticism of the first formulation of the categorical imperative: that one can manipulate the imperative to get the results one wishes by framing the maxim appropriately.

Even if Levitt's account is perfectly accurate, however, the second major statement of the imperative still creates problems for manipulative advertising. Here, the question seems to boil down to the following: are firms that employ manipulative advertising using a consumer merely as a means to their own ends and therefore violating the imperative if the consumer, in effect, needs and wants to be manipulated? If, as I suggested earlier, the suspension of disbelief required for one to accept manipulative advertising may be more or less reasonable, then advertisers conceivably *are* respecting consumers' rationality by providing them with product-related illusions. . . .

VIRTUE ETHICS

Earlier I depicted Galbraith as a utilitarian, but other moral aspirations probably were at work within *The Affluent Society*. The book opened with the following quotation from Alfred Marshall: "The economist, like everyone else, must concern himself with the ultimate aims of man." Galbraith's conviction that consumerism does not rank high among those aims pervades much of his writing, and almost certainly informed his critique of advertising. However, the ethical values and theories previously considered in this article do not state and enjoin the desirable substantive conditions of human life. . . .

Waide's alternative to such approaches is to examine "the virtues and vices at stake" in manipulative advertising (1987, 73), and to see "what kinds of lives are sustained" by it (77). Stanley Benn sounds the same note when he suggests that the key question about advertising is whether it promotes "a valuable kind of life," with this determination depending on "some objective assessment of what constitutes excellence in human beings" (1967, 273). Because manipulative advertising encourages advertisers to ignore the well-being of their targets and encourages those targets to neglect the cultivation of nonmarket goods, Waide concludes that it makes us less virtuous persons and therefore is morally objectionable (1987, 74–75). Many other critics of advertising make the same general point. . . . Heilbroner called advertising "perhaps the single most value-destroying activity of a business civilization," due to the "subversive influence of the relentless effort to persuade people to change their lifeways, not out of any knowledge of, or deeply held convictions about the 'good life,' but merely to sell whatever article or service is being pandered" (1976, 113–14). His main specific complaint is that by offering a constant stream of half-truths and deceptions, advertising makes "cynics of us all" (114). Virginia Held makes a related point when she criticizes advertising for undermining intellectual and artistic integrity (1984, 64–66).

To Christopher Lasch, on the other hand, advertising's greatest evil may be its tendency to leave consumers "perpetually unsatisfied, restless, anxious, and bored" (1978, 72). . . . One suspects that Lasch might reject advertising's consequences as inherently bad even if they did mark an increase in utility. The same probably holds for most of advertising's cultural critics. As a group, Michael Schudson remarks, they see "the emergence of a consumer culture as a devolution of manners, morals and even manhood, from a work-oriented production ethic of the past to the consumption, 'lifestyle'-obsessed, ethic-less pursuits of the present" (1984, 6–7).

Uniting all these varied criticisms of advertising is the notion that it promotes substantive behaviors, experiences, and states of character which are inherently undesirable, and that it is morally objectionable for this reason. . . . This article assumes that manipulative advertising both creates a consumer culture and strongly influences individual purchase decisions. Its main means for accomplishing the second aim (and perhaps the first) is to associate the product with such nonmarket goods as sex, status, and power. On those assumptions, manipulative advertising almost certainly undermines such standard virtues as honesty and benevolence in its practitioners, and arguably dilutes its targets' moderation, reasonableness, self-control, self-discipline, and self-reliance (Rachels 1993, 163 [listing these virtues]). . . .

MANIPULATIVE ADVERTISING'S LAST DEFENSE

All things considered, virtue ethics appears to be the best basis for attacking manipulative advertising. In particular, it seems to dispose of a defense that has plagued our other three attacks on such advertising: Levitt's claim that people want and need advertising's illusions and therefore more or less knowingly and willingly embrace it. Like our other bases for attacking manipulative advertising, however, virtue ethics is not assumed to be an absolute. This might mean that the claims of virtue would have to give way if human beings simply could not endure without advertising's illusions or if its psychic satisfactions give people enormous amounts of utility.

In any event, there is yet another possible defense of manipulative advertising. This defense is mainly utilitarian, but it also implicates my other three ethical criteria to some degree. It arises because by hypothesis all my criteria must be weighed against competing moral claims. The defense does not so much challenge the assertion that manipulative advertising is bad, as argue that it is the lesser of two evils.

Throughout this article, I have assumed for the sake of argument that manipulative advertising's critics are correct in their assessment of its effects. As we have seen, these people usually maintain that manipulative advertising plays an important role in socializing people to consume. This means that on the critics' view of things, manipulative advertising is central to the functioning of modern consumer society. But if manipulative advertising is central to the system's operation, how safely can it be condemned? Assuming that the condemnation is effective, manipulative advertising disappears, and all advertising becomes informative, people gradually would be weaned from their consumerist ways. This is likely to create social instability, with a more authoritarian form of government the likely end result. That, in turn, could well mean an environment in which aggregate utility is lower than it is today, human autonomy and rational nature are less respected, and/or the virtues less recognized.

One set of reasons for these conclusions is largely economic. If people become less consumerist as manipulative advertising leaves the scene, aggregate demand and economic output should decline. At first glance, this would seem to be of little consequence because by hypothesis people would value material things less. The problem is that the economic losses probably will be unevenly distributed: for example, some businesses will fail and some will not, and some people will lose their jobs while others stay employed. These inequalities are a potential source of social instability. Both to redress them and to preserve order, government is likely to intervene. This may involve a significant increase in outright governmental coercion. . . .

To my knowledge, Waide is the only business ethicist to raise these kinds of problems, and he finds himself without a solution to them. Because "[i]t seems unlikely that [manipulative] advertising will end suddenly," however, Waide is "confident that we will have the time and the imagination to adapt our economy to do without it" (1987, 77). Although I suspect that Waide is too optimistic, I have no solution to the dilemma either. Thus, I am left with the unsatisfactory conclusion that while various moral arguments may provide sound bases for attacking manipulative advertising, prudential considerations dictate that none of them be pressed too vigorously. Manipulative advertising's ultimate justification, in other words, may be its status as a necessary evil.

CONCLUDING REMARKS

For all the preceding reasons, it seems that there is no completely definitive basis for condemning manipulative advertising. But this obviously is not to say that the practice is morally unproblematic. Of my four suggested attacks on the practice, virtue ethics seems the strongest, with Kantianism a close second, autonomy third, and utilitarianism last. Indeed, utilitarianism may even support manipulative advertising. The main reason is that the practice's three most important defenses—Levitt's argument, the assertion that there is little connection between a want's origin outside the individual and the benefit resulting from its satisfaction, and manipulative advertising's centrality to our economic system—are more or less utilitarian in nature.

Except perhaps for hard-core utilitarians, therefore, manipulative advertising is a morally dubious practice. However, this conclusion may depend heavily on a critical assumption made earlier: that manipulative advertising actually works. Specifically, I assumed that such advertising: (1) socializes people to adopt a consumerist lifestyle, and (2) strongly influences individual purchase decisions. But what happens if, by and large, each assumption is untrue?

On first impressions, at least, it appears that if manipulative advertising is inefficacious, utilitarianism, autonomy, and virtue ethics largely cease to be bases for criticizing it. . . .

However, Kantian objections to manipulative advertising might well remain even if it is inefficacious. On that assumption, admittedly, perhaps one would will the universalization of a maxim permitting such advertising. If manipulative advertising simply fails to work, moreover, maybe it does not treat consumers merely as means to advertiser's ends. But such arguments ignore the strong anticonsequentialism of Kant's ethics, which arguably renders advertising's ineffectiveness irrelevant. More importantly, those arguments ignore Kant's stress on the motives with which people should act. The only thing that is unqualifiedly good, Kant says, is a good will; and the good will is good not because of what it accomplishes, but simply because it wills the good (Kant 1964, 61–62). Even if manipulative advertising is unsuccessful, advertisers presumably try to make it work. Unless they believe that their efforts would benefit consumers in the end, it is unlikely that they are acting with a good will when they devise and employ their stratagems.

At a first cut, therefore, it seems that if manipulative advertising is ineffective, the only significant ethical objections to it are Kantian. (To these we might add the money wasted on the practice, as well as its effect on the virtue of its practitioners.) For those inclined to ignore Kantian objections, therefore, it seems that manipulative advertising's rightness or wrongness depends less on ethical theory than on empirical questions within the purview of the social sciences. . . . As the preceding discussion suggests, the most important such question is the extent to which manipulative advertising actually affects purchase decisions and socializes people to consume. Even if manipulative advertising actually has those effects, other more or less empirical issues would remain. These include the validity of Levitt's arguments, Galbraith's asserted connection between a desire's origin outside the individual and the low utility resulting from its satisfaction, and manipulative advertising's contribution to gross domestic product. All these questions, I submit, are unlikely to be answered any time soon. . . .

NOTES

1. However, I do not consider the "everyone's doing it" defense. On this subject, see Ronald M. Green, "When Is 'Everyone's Doing It' a Moral Justification?" *Business Ethics Quarterly* 1, no. 1: 75–93. [Reprinted in this volume.]

REFERENCES

Benn, S. (1967) "Freedom and persuasion." *The Australasian Journal of Philosophy* 45: 259–75.

Galbraith, J. K. (1958) *The Affluent Society* (Boston: Houghton Mifflin).

Genge, W. (1985) "Ads stimulate the economy." *Business and Society Review* 1, no. 55: 58–59.

Hare, R. M. (1984) "Commentary." *Business and Professional Ethics Journal* 3, nos. 3 & 4: 23–28.

Hayek, F. A. (1961) "The *non sequitur* of the 'dependence effect.'" *Southern Economic Journal* 27: 346–48.

Heilbroner, R. (1976) *Business Civilization in Decline* (New York: W.W. Norton).

Held, V. (1984) "Advertising and program content." *Business and Professional Ethics Journal* 3, nos. 3 & 4: 61–76.

Kant, I. (1964) *Groundwork of the Metaphysic of Morals* (New York: Harper Torchbook, H. J. Paton tr.).

Lasch, C. (1978) *The Culture of Narcissism: American Life in An Age of Diminishing Expectations* (New York: W.W. Norton).

Levitt, T. (1970). "The morality (?) of advertising." *Harvard Business Review* (July-August): 84–92.

Lippke, R. (1990) "Advertising and the social conditions of autonomy." *Business and Professional Ethics Journal* 8, no. 4: 35–58.

Lukes, S. (1973) *Individualism* (Oxford: Basil Blackwell).

Rachels, J. (1993) *The Elements of Moral Philosophy* (New York: McGraw-Hill, 2nd ed.).

Schudson, M. (1986). *Advertising, The Uneasy Persuasion: Its Dubious Impact on American Society* (New York: Basic Books, 2nd ed.).

Waide, J. (1987) "The making of self and world in advertising." *Journal of Business Ethics* 6, no. 2: 73–79.

REVIEW AND DISCUSSION QUESTIONS

1. Give examples of advertisements that you consider manipulative. Does advertising socialize people to a life of consumption? To what extent does it influence or even dictate our individual brand and product choices?

2. Assess Galbraith's contention that because advertising induces or creates consumer wants, those wants are not urgent and their satisfaction does not generate much utility.

3. Is Levitt correct that consumers need and want the illusions of advertising? Is it true that as consumers we are not only buying a physical product, but also a set of positive feelings connected with it by advertising? Would you agree with Levitt that "embellishment and distortion are among advertising's legitimate and socially desirable purposes"? Do the promises and images of advertising bring us genuine satisfaction?

4. Assuming that manipulative advertising is effective, does it undermine one's autonomy? Does it promote undesirable behaviors and character traits, as the virtue-ethics critique alleges?
5. Assess the argument that manipulative advertising is a necessary evil because it is central to the continued functioning of our socioeconomic system. In your view, does advertising play a positive or negative role in our society?
6. Is manipulative advertising wrong? What do you see as the strongest ethical argument against it? Suppose manipulative advertising doesn't work. Would it still be wrong?

SUGGESTIONS FOR FURTHER READING

Two early and influential contributions to the debate over advertising are John Kenneth Galbraith, *The Affluent Society* (Houghton Mifflin 1959), and Theodore Levitt, "The Morality (?) of Advertising," *Harvard Business Review* 48 (July-August 1970). Other important discussions are Robert L. Arrington, "Advertising and Behavior Control," *Journal of Business Ethics* 1 (February 1982); John Waide, "The Making of Self and World in Advertising," *Journal of Business Ethics* 6 (February 1987); Roger Crisp, "Persuasive Advertising, Autonomy, and the Creation of Desire," *Journal of Business Ethics* 6 (July 1987); Richard L. Lippke, "Advertising and the Social Conditions of Autonomy," *Business and Professional Ethics Journal* 8 (Winter 1989); and Andrew Gustafson, "Advertising's Impact on Morality in Society: Influencing Habits and Desires of Consumers," *Business and Society Review* 106 (Fall 2001).

CHAPTER TEN

What Is Really Unethical About Insider Trading?

Jennifer Moore

In the United States and most developed countries, insider trading is illegal, but not everyone agrees that it is morally wrong or that it ought to be outlawed. And those who do believe that it is wrong often give different reasons for thinking so. In this essay, Jennifer Moore, professor of law at the University of Wisconsin, examines the three most common arguments against insider trading: that the practice is unfair, that it involves a "misappropriation" of information, and that it harms ordinary investors. She criticizes each of these arguments, concluding that none of them suffices to show that insider trading is unethical and should be illegal. Instead, she argues that what is really wrong about insider trading, and the real reason for prohibiting it, is that it undermines the fiduciary relationship that lies at the heart of business management.

THINGS TO CONSIDER
1. Distinguish the "equal information" version and the "equal access" version of the fairness argument against insider trading.
2. Explain the "property rights" or "misappropriation" argument against insider trading.
3. What are the two harm-based arguments against insider trading?
4. What is a fiduciary relationship? Are such relationships important in business? Give an example.
5. Moore identifies four situations in which insider trading would not benefit the firm. What are they?

From *Journal of Business Ethics* 9 (March 1990). Copyright © 1990 by D. Reidel Publishing Co. Reprinted by permission of Kluwer Academic Publishers. Some notes omitted.

This paper is divided into two parts. In the first part, I examine critically the principal ethical arguments against insider trading. The arguments fall into three main classes: arguments based on fairness, arguments based on property rights in information, and arguments based on harm to ordinary investors or the market as a whole. Each of these arguments, I contend, has some serious deficiencies. No one of them by itself provides a sufficient reason for outlawing insider trading. This does not mean, however, that there are no reasons for prohibiting the practice. Once we have cleared away the inadequate arguments, other, more cogent reasons for outlawing insider trading come to light. In the second part of the paper, I set out what I take to be the real reasons for laws against insider trading.

The term *insider trading* needs some preliminary clarification. Both the SEC and the courts have strongly resisted pressure to define the notion clearly. In 1961, the SEC stated that corporate insiders—such as officers or directors—in possession of material, nonpublic information were required to disclose that information or to refrain from trading. But this "disclose or refrain" rule has since been extended to persons other than corporate insiders. People who get information from insiders ("tippees") and those who become "temporary insiders" in the course of some work they perform for the company, can acquire the duty of insiders in some cases. Financial printers and newspaper columnists, not "insiders" in the technical sense, have also been found guilty of insider trading. Increasingly, the term *insider* has come to refer to the kind of information a person possesses rather than to the status of the person who trades on that information. My use of the term will reflect this ambiguity. In this paper, an "insider trader" is someone who trades in material, nonpublic information—not necessarily a corporate insider.

1. ETHICAL ARGUMENTS AGAINST INSIDER TRADING

Fairness

Probably the most common reason given for thinking that insider trading is unethical is that it is "unfair." For proponents of the fairness argument, the key feature of insider trading is the disparity of information between the two parties to the transaction. Trading should take place on a "level playing field," they argue, and disparities in information tilt the field toward one player and away from the other. There are two versions of the fairness argument: the first argues that insider trading is unfair because the two parties do not have *equal* information; the second argues that insider trading is unfair because the two parties do not have equal *access* to information. Let us look at the two versions one at a time.

According to the equal information argument, insider trading is unfair because one party to the transaction lacks information the other party has, and is thus at a disadvantage. Although this is a very strict notion of fairness, it has its proponents, and hints of this view appear in some of the judicial opinions. One proponent of the equal information argument is Saul Levmore, who claims that "fairness is achieved when insiders and outsiders are in equal positions. That is, a system is fair if we would not expect one group to envy the position of the other." As thus defined, Levmore claims, fairness "reflects the 'golden rule' of impersonal behavior—treating others as we would ourselves."[1] If Levmore is correct, then not just insider trading, but *all* transactions in which there is a disparity of information are unfair, and thus unethical. But this claim seems overly broad. An example will help to illustrate some of the problems with it.

Suppose I am touring Vermont and come across an antique blanket chest in the barn of a farmer, a chest I know will bring $2,500 back in the city. I offer to buy it for $75, and the farmer agrees. If he had known how much I could get for it back home, he probably would have asked a higher price—but I failed to disclose this information. I have profited from an informational advantage. Have I been unethical? My suspicion is that most people would say I have not. While knowing how much I could sell the chest for in the city is in the interest of the farmer, I am not morally obligated to reveal it. I am not morally obligated to tell those who deal with me *everything* that it would be in their interest to know. . . .

In general, it is only when I owe a *duty* to the other party that I am legally required to reveal all information that is in his interest. In such a situation, the other party believes that I am looking out for his interests, and I deceive him if I do not do so. Failure to disclose is deceptive in this instance because of the relationship of trust and dependence between the parties. But this suggests that trading on inside information is wrong, *not* because it violates a general notion of fairness, but because a breach of fiduciary duty is involved. Cases of insider trading in which no fiduciary duty of this kind is breached would not be unethical. . . .

The "equal information" version of the fairness argument seems to me to fail. However, it could be argued that insider trading is unfair because the insider has information that is not *accessible* to the ordinary investor. For proponents of this second type of fairness argument, it is not the insider's information advantage that counts, but the fact that this advantage is "unerodable," one that cannot be overcome by the hard work and ingenuity of the ordinary investor. No matter how hard the latter works, he is unable to acquire nonpublic information, because this information is protected by law.[2]

This type of fairness argument seems more promising, since it allows people to profit from informational advantages of their own making, but not from advantages that are built into the system. Proponents of this "equal access" argument would probably find my deal with the Vermont farmer unobjectionable, because information about antiques is not in principle unavailable to the farmer. The problem with the argument is that the notion of "equal access" is not very clear. What does it mean for two people to have equal access to information?

Suppose my pipes are leaking and I call a plumber to fix them. He charges me for the job, and benefits by the informational advantage he has over me. Most of us would not find this transaction unethical. True, I don't have "equal access" to the information needed to fix my pipes in any real sense, but I could have had this information had I chosen to become a plumber. The disparity of information in this case is simply something that is built into the fact that people choose to specialize in different areas. But just as I could have chosen to become a plumber, I could have chosen to become a corporate insider with access to legally protected information. . . .

One might argue that I have easier access to a plumber's information than I do to an insider trader's, since there are lots of plumbers from whom I can buy the information I seek. The fact that insiders have a strong incentive to keep their information to themselves is a serious objection to insider trading. But if insider trading were made legal, insiders could profit not only from trading on their information, but also on selling it to willing buyers. Proponents of the practice argue that a brisk market in information would soon develop—indeed, it might be argued that such a market already exists, though in illegal and clandestine form.[3] . . .

The most interesting thing about the fairness argument is not that it provides a compelling reason to outlaw insider trading, but that it leads to issues we cannot settle on the basis of an abstract concept of fairness alone. The claim that parties to a transaction should have equal information, or equal access to information, inevitably raises questions about how informational advantages are (or should be) acquired, and when people are entitled to use them for profit. . . .

Property Rights in Information

As economists and legal scholars have recognized, information is a valuable thing, and it is possible to view it as a type of property. We already treat certain types of information as property: trade secrets, inventions, and so on—and protect them by law. Proponents of the property rights argument claim that material, nonpublic information is also a kind of property, and that insider trading is wrong because it involves a violation of property rights.

If inside information is a kind of property, whose property is it? How does information come to belong to one person rather than another? This is a very complex question, because information differs in many ways from other, more tangible sorts of property. But one influential argument is that information belongs to the people who discover, originate, or "create" it. As Bill Shaw put it in a recent article, "the originator of the information (the individual or corporation that spent hard-earned bucks producing it) owns and controls this asset just as it does other proprietary goods."[4] Thus, if a firm agrees to a deal, invents a new product, or discovers new natural resources, it has a property right in that information and is entitled to exclusive use of it for its own profit.

It is important to note that it is the firm itself (and/or its shareholders), and not the individual employees of the firm, who have property rights in the information. To be sure, it is always certain individuals in the firm who put together the deal, invent the product, or discover the resources. But they are able to do this only because they are backed by the power and authority of the firm. The employees of the firm—managers, officers, directors—are not entitled to the information any more than they are entitled to corporate trade secrets or patents on products that they develop for the firm. It is the firm that makes it possible to create the information and that makes the information valuable once it has been created. As Victor Brudney puts it,

> The insiders have acquired the information at the expense of the enterprise, and for the purpose of conducting the business for the collective good of all the stockholders, entirely apart from personal benefits from trading in its securities. There is no reason for them to be entitled to trade for their own benefit on the basis of such information . . .[5]

If this analysis is correct, then it suggests that insider trading is wrong because it is a form of theft. It is not exactly like theft, because the person who uses inside information does not deprive the company of the use of the information. But he does deprive the company of the *sole* use of the information, which is itself an asset. The insider trader "misappropriates," as the laws puts it, information that belongs to the company and uses it in a way in which it was not intended—for personal profit. It is not surprising that this "misappropriation theory" has begun to take hold in the courts, and has become one of the predominant rationales in prosecuting insider trading cases. In *U.S. v. Newman,* a case involving investment bankers and securities traders, for example, the court stated:

> In *U.S. v. Chiarella,* Chief Justice Burger . . . said that the defendant "misappropriated"—stole to put it bluntly—"valuable nonpublic information entrusted to him in the utmost confidence." That characterization aptly describes the conduct of the connivers in the instant case. . . . By sullying the reputations of [their] employers as safe repositories of client confidences, appellee and his cohorts defrauded those employers as surely as if they took their money.[6]

The misappropriation theory also played a major role in the prosecution of R. Foster Winans, a *Wall Street Journal* reporter who traded on and leaked to others the contents of his "Heard on the Street" column.[7]

This theory is quite persuasive, as far as it goes. But it is not enough to show that insider trading is always unethical or that it should be illegal. If insider information is really the property of the firm that produces it, then using that property is wrong *only when the firm prohibits it.* If the firm does not prohibit insider trading, it seems perfectly acceptable.* Most companies do in fact forbid insider trading. But it is not clear whether they do so because they don't want their employees using corporate property for profit or simply because it is illegal. Proponents of insider trading point out that most corporations did not prohibit insider trading until recently, when it became a prime concern of enforcement agencies. . . .

A crucial factor here would be the shareholders' agreement to allow insider information. Shareholders may not wish to allow trading on inside information because they may wish the employees of the company to be devoted simply to advancing shareholder interests. We will return to this point below. But if shareholders did allow it, it would seem to be permissible. Still others argue that shareholders would not need to "agree" in any way other than to be told this information when they were buying the stock. If they did not want to hold stock in a company whose employees were permitted to trade in inside information, they would not buy that stock. Hence they could be said to have "agreed."

Manne and other proponents of insider trading have suggested a number of reasons why "shareholders would voluntarily enter into contractual arrangements with insiders giving them property rights in valuable information."[8] Their principal argument is that permitting insider trading would serve as an incentive to create more information—put together more deals, invent more new products, or make more discoveries. Such an incentive, they argue, would create more profit for shareholders in the long run. Assigning employees the right to trade on inside information could take the place of more traditional (and expensive) elements in the employee's compensation package. Rather than giving out end of the year bonuses, for example, firms could allow employees to put together their own bonuses by cashing in on inside information, thus saving the company money. In addition, proponents argue, insider trading would improve the efficiency of the market. We will return to these claims below.

If inside information really is a form of corporate property, firms

---

*Unless there is some other reason for forbidding it, such as that it harms others. See [the following section].

may assign employees the right to trade on it if they choose to do so. The only reason for not permitting firms to allow employees to trade on their information would be that doing so causes harm to other investors or to society at large. Although our society values property rights very highly, they are not absolute. We do not hesitate to restrict property rights if their exercise causes significant harm to others. The permissibility of insider trading, then, ultimately seems to depend on whether the practice is harmful.

Harm

There are two principal harm-based arguments against insider trading. The first claims that the practice is harmful to ordinary investors who engage in trades with insiders; the second claims that insider trading erodes investors' confidence in the market, causing them to pull out of the market and harming the market as a whole. I will address the two arguments in turn.

Although proponents of insider trading often refer to it as a "victimless crime," implying that no one is harmed by it, it is not difficult to think of examples of transactions with insiders in which ordinary investors are made worse off. Suppose I have placed an order with my broker to sell my shares in Megalith Co., currently trading at $50 a share, at $60 or above. An insider knows that Behemoth Inc. is going to announce a tender offer for Megalith shares in two days, and has begun to buy large amounts of stock in anticipation of the gains. Because of his market activity, Megalith stock rises to $65 a share and my order is triggered. If he had refrained from trading, the price would have risen steeply two days later, and I would have been able to sell my shares for $80. Because the insider traded, I failed to realize the gains that I otherwise would have made.

But there are other examples of transactions in which ordinary investors *benefit* from insider trading. Suppose I tell my broker to sell my shares in Acme Corp., currently trading at $45, if the price drops to $40 or lower. An insider knows of an enormous class action suit to be brought against Acme in two days. He sells his shares, lowering the price to $38 and triggering my sale. When the suit is made public two days later, the share price plunges to $25. If the insider had abstained from trading, I would have lost far more than I did. Here, the insider has protected me from loss. . . .

The truth about an ordinary investor's gains and losses from trading with insiders seems to be not that insider trading is never harmful, but that it is not systematically or consistently harmful. Insider trading is not a "victimless crime," as its proponents claim, but it is often difficult to tell exactly who the victims are and to what extent they have been victimized. The stipulation of the law to "disclose *or* abstain" from trading makes determining victims even more complex. While some investors are harmed by the insider's trade, to others the insider's actions make no difference at all; what harms them is simply *not having complete information* about the stock in question. Forbidding insider trading will not prevent these harms. Investors who neither buy nor sell, or who buy or sell for reasons independent of share price, fall into this category.

Permitting insider trading would undoubtedly make the securities market *riskier* for ordinary investors. Even proponents of the practice seem to agree with this claim. But if insider trading were permitted openly, they argue, investors would compensate for the extra riskiness by demanding a discount in share price.[9] . . . If insider trading were permitted, in short, we could expect a general drop in share prices, but no net harm to investors would result. Moreover, improved efficiency would result in a bigger pie for everyone. These are empirical claims, and I am not equipped to determine if they are true. If they are, however, they would defuse one of the most important objections to insider trading, and provide a powerful argument for leaving the control of inside information up to individual corporations.

The second harm-based argument claims that permitting insider trading would cause ordinary investors to lose confidence in the market and cease to invest there, thus harming the market as a whole. As former SEC Chairman John Shad puts it, "if people get the impression that they're playing against a marked deck, they're simply not going to be willing to invest."[10] Since capital markets play a crucial role in allocating resources in our economy, this objection is a very serious one.

The weakness of the argument is that it turns almost exclusively on the *feelings* or *perceptions* of ordinary investors, and does not address the question of whether these perceptions are justified. If permitting insider trading really does harm ordinary investors, then this "loss of confidence" argument becomes a compelling reason for outlawing insider trading. But if, as many claim, the practice does not harm ordinary investors, then the sensible course of action is to educate the investors, not to outlaw insider trading. It is irrational to cater to the feelings of ordinary investors if those feelings are not justified. We ought not to outlaw perfectly permissible actions just because some people feel (unjustifiably) disadvantaged by them. More research is needed to determine the actual impact of insider trading on the ordinary investor.[11]

II.   Is There Anything Wrong with Insider Trading?

My contention has been that the principal ethical arguments against insider trading do not, by themselves, suffice to show that the practice is unethical and should be illegal. The strongest arguments are those that turn on the notion of a fiduciary duty to act in the interest of shareholders, or on the idea of inside information as company "property." But in both arguments, the impermissibility of insider trading depends on a contractual understanding among the company, its shareholders and its employees. In both cases, a modification of this understanding could change the moral status of insider trading.

Does this mean that there is nothing wrong with insider trading? No. If insider trading is unethical, it is so *in the context* of the relationship among the firm, its shareholders, and its employees. It is possible to change this context in a way that makes the practice permissible. But *should* the context be changed? I will argue that it should not. Because it threatens the fiduciary relationship that is central to business management, I believe, permitting insider trading is in the interest neither of the firm, its shareholders, nor society at large.

Fiduciary relationships are relationships of trust and dependence in which one party acts in the interest of another. They appear in many contexts, but are absolutely essential to conducting business in a complex society. Fiduciary relationships allow parties with different resources, skills, and information to cooperate in productive activity. Shareholders who wish to invest in a business, for example, but who cannot or do not wish to run it themselves, hire others to manage it for them. Managers, directors, and to some extent, other employees, become fiduciaries for the firms they manage and for the shareholders of those firms.

The fiduciary relationship is one of moral and legal obligation.

Fiduciaries, that is, are bound to act in the interests of those who depend on them even if these interests do not coincide with their own. Typically, however, fiduciary relationships are constructed as far as possible so that the interests of the fiduciaries and the parties for whom they act *do* coincide. Where the interests of the two parties compete or conflict, the fiduciary relationship is threatened. . . .

Significantly, proponents of insider trading do not dispute the importance of the fiduciary relationship. Rather, they argue that permitting insider trading would *increase* the likelihood that employees will act in the interest of shareholders and their firms.[12] We have already touched on the main argument for this claim. Manne and others contend that assigning employees the right to trade on inside information would provide a powerful incentive for creative and entrepreneurial activity. It would encourage new inventions, creative deals, and efficient new management practices, thus increasing the profits, strength, and overall competitiveness of the firm. Manne goes so far as to argue that permission to trade on insider information is the only appropriate way to compensate entrepreneurial activity, and warns: "[I]f no way to reward the entrepreneur within a corporation exists, he will tend to disappear from the corporate scene."[13] The entrepreneur makes an invaluable contribution to the firm and its shareholders, and his disappearance would no doubt cause serious harm.

If permitting insider trading is to work in the way proponents suggest, however, there must be a direct and consistent link between the profits reaped by insider traders and the performance that benefits the firm. It is not at all clear that this is the case—indeed, there is evidence that the opposite is true. There appear to be many ways to profit from inside information that do not benefit the firm at all. I mention four possibilities below. Two of these (2 and 3) are simply ways in which insider traders can profit without benefiting the firm, suggesting that permitting insider trading is a poor incentive for performance and fails firmly to link the interests of managers, directors, and employees to those of the corporation as a whole. The others (1 and 4) are actually harmful to the corporation, setting up conflicts of interest and actively undermining the fiduciary relationship.

1. Proponents of insider trading tend to speak as if all information were positive. "Information," in the proponents' lexicon, always con-

cerns a creative new deal, a new, efficient way of conducting business, or a new product. If this were true, allowing trades on inside information might provide an incentive to work even harder for the good of the company. But information can also concern *bad* news—a large lawsuit, an unsafe or poor quality product, or lower-than-expected performance. Such negative information can be just as valuable to the insider trader as positive information. If the freedom to trade on positive information encourages acts that are beneficial to the firm, then by the same reasoning the freedom to trade on negative information would encourage harmful acts. At the very least, permitting employees to profit from harms to the company decreases the incentive to avoid such harms. Permission to trade on negative inside information gives rise to inevitable conflicts of interest. Proponents of insider trading have not satisfactorily answered this objection.[14]

2. Proponents of insider trading also assume that the easiest way to profit on inside information is to "create" it. But it is not at all clear that this is true. Putting together a deal, inventing a new product, and other productive activities that add value to the firm usually require a significant investment of time and energy. For the well-placed employee, it would be far easier to start a rumor that the company has a new product or is about to announce a deal than to sit down and produce either one—and it would be just as profitable for the employee. If permitting insider trading provides an incentive for the productive "creation" of information, it seems to provide an even greater incentive for the nonproductive "invention" of information, or stock manipulation. The invention of information is in the interest neither of the firm nor of society at large.

3. Even if negative or false information did not pose problems, the incentive argument for insider trading overlooks the difficulties posed by "free riders"—those who do not actually contribute to the creation of the information, but who are nevertheless aware of it and can profit by trading on it. . . . Unless those who do not contribute can be excluded from trading on it, there will be no incentive to produce the desired information; it will not get created at all.

4. Finally, allowing trading on inside information would tend to deflect employees' attention from the day-to-day business of running the company and focus it on major changes, positive or negative, that lead to large insider trading profits. This might not be true if one could profit by inside information about the day-to-day efficiency of the operation, a continuous tradition of product quality, or a consistently lean operating budget. But these things do not generate the kind of information on which insider traders can reap large profits. Insider profits come from dramatic changes, from "news"—not from steady, long-term performance. If the firm and its shareholders have a genuine interest in such performance, then permitting insider trading creates a conflict of interest for insiders. The ability to trade on inside information is also likely to influence the types of information officers announce to the public, and the timing of such announcements, making it less likely that the information and its timing is optimal for the firm. And the problems of false or negative information remain.[15]

If the arguments given above are correct, permitting insider trading does not increase the likelihood that insiders will act in the interest of the firm and its shareholders. In some cases, it actually causes conflicts of interest, undermining the fiduciary relationship essential to managing the corporation. This claim, in turn, gives corporations good reason to prohibit the practice. But insider trading remains primarily a private matter among corporations, shareholders, and employees. It is appropriate to ask why, given this fact about insider trading, the practice should be *illegal*. If it is primarily corporate and shareholder interests that are threatened by insider trading, why not let corporations themselves bear the burden of enforcement? Why involve the SEC? There are two possible reasons for continuing to support laws against insider trading. The first is that even if they wish to prohibit insider trading, individual corporations do not have the resources to do so effectively. The second is that society itself has a stake in the fiduciary relationship. . . .

The notion of the fiduciary duty owed by managers and other employees to the firm and its shareholders has a long and venerable history in our society. Nearly all of our important activities require some sort of cooperation, trust, or reliance on others, and the ability of one person to act in the interest of another—as a fiduciary—is central to this cooperation. The role of managers as fiduciaries for firms and shareholders is grounded in the property rights of shareholders. They are the owners of the firm, and bear the residual risks, and hence have a right to have it managed in their interest. The fiduciary relationship also contributes to efficiency, since it encourages those who are willing to take risks to place their resources in the hands of those who have the expertise to maximize their usefulness. While this "shareholder theory" of the firm has often been challenged in recent years, this has been primarily by people who argue that the fiduciary concept should be widened to include other "stakeholders" in the firm. I have heard no one argue that the notion of managers' fiduciary duties should be eliminated entirely, and that managers should begin working primarily for themselves.

III.   CONCLUSION

I have argued that the real reason for prohibiting insider trading is that it erodes the fiduciary relationship that lies at the heart of our business organizations. The more frequently heard moral arguments based on fairness, property rights in information, and harm to ordinary investors, are not compelling. Of these, the fairness arguments seem to me the least persuasive. The claim that a trader must reveal everything that it is in the interest of another party to know, seems to hold up only when the other is someone to whom he owes a fiduciary duty. But this is not really a "fairness" argument at all. Similarly, the "misappropriation" theory is only persuasive if we can offer reasons for corporations not to assign the right to trade on inside information to their employees. I have found these in the fact that permitting insider trading threatens the fiduciary relationship. I do believe that lifting the ban against insider trading would cause harms to shareholders, corporations, and society at large. But again, these harms stem primarily from the cracks in the fiduciary relationship caused by permitting insider trading, rather than from actual trades with insiders. Violation of fiduciary duty, in short, is at the center of insider trading offenses.

NOTES

1. Saul Levmore, "Securities and Secrets: Insider Trading and the Law of Contracts," 68 *Virginia Law Review* 117.
2. The equal access argument is perhaps best stated by Victor Brudney in his influential article, "Insiders, Outsiders and Informational Advantages Under the Federal Securities Laws," 93 *Harvard Law Review* 322.
3. Manne, *Insider Trading and the Stock Market* (Free Press, New York, 1966), 75.
4. Bill Shaw, "Should Insider Trading Be Outside the Law?" *Business and Soci-*

ety Review 66: 34. See also Macey, "From Fairness to Contract: The New Direction of the Rules Against Insider Trading," 13 *Hofstra Law Review* 9 (1984).

5. Brudney, "Insiders, Outsiders, and Informational Advantages," 344.
6. *U.S. v. Newman,* 664 F. 2d 17.
7. *U.S. v. Winans,* 612 F. Supp. 827. The Supreme Court upheld Winans's conviction, but was evenly split on the misappropriation theory. As a consequence, the Supreme Court has still not truly endorsed the theory, although several lower court decisions have been based on it. . . .
8. Carlton and Fischel, "The Regulation of Insider Trading," 35 *Stanford Law Review* 857. See also Manne, *Insider Trading and the Stock Market.*
9. Kenneth Scott, "Insider Trading: Rule 10b-5, Disclosure and Corporate Privacy," 9 *Journal of Legal Studies* 808.
10. "Disputes Arise Over Value of Laws on Insider Trading," *The Wall Street Journal,* November 17, 1986, 28.
11. One area that needs more attention is the impact of insider trading on the markets (and ordinary investors) of countries that permit the practice. Proponents of insider trading are fond of pointing out that insider trading has been legal in many overseas markets for years, without the dire effects predicted by opponents of the practice. Opponents reply that these markets are not as fair or efficient as U.S. markets, or that they do not play as important a role in the allocation of capital.
12. See Frank Easterbrook, "Insider Trading as an Agency Problem," *Principals and Agents: The Structure of Business* (Cambridge, MA: Harvard University Press, 1985). I speak here as if the interests of the firm and its shareholders are identical, even though this is sometimes not the case.
13. Manne, *Insider Trading and the Stock Market,* 129.
14. Manne is aware of the "bad news" objection, but he glosses over it by claiming that bad news is not as likely as good news to provide large gains for insider traders. *Insider Trading and the Stock Market,* 102.
15. There are ways to avoid many of these objections. For example, Manne has suggested "isolating" non-contributors so that they cannot trade on the information produced by others. Companies could also forbid trading on "negative" information. The problem is that these piecemeal restrictions seem very costly—more costly than simply prohibiting insider trading as we do now. In addition, each restriction brings us farther and farther away from what proponents of the practice actually want: unrestricted insider trading.

REVIEW AND DISCUSSION QUESTIONS

1. Do you find Moore's critique of the fairness argument convincing, or is there something unfair or unethical about transactions between parties that lack equal information or equal access to information?
2. If insider trading were legal, then it would be up to individual companies and their shareholders to decide whether to permit it. Would

it be in their interest to permit inside trading? Explain why or why not.
3. Is insider trading a "victimless crime?" Does it harm ordinary investors? Would permitting it erode investors' confidence in the stock market?
4. Would permitting insider trading have good results or bad results for firms? Would it weaken or even undermine the fiduciary relationship that Moore believes lies at the heart of business management?
5. Has Moore neglected any pertinent arguments or considerations either for or against insider trading? Do you believe that insider trading is wrong? Do you believe that it should remain illegal?

SUGGESTIONS FOR FURTHER READING

Tibor Machan, "What is Morally Right with Insider Trading," *Public Affairs Quarterly* 10 (April 1996) provides a succinct, libertarian defense of insider trading, while Patricia H. Werhane argues against it in "The Ethics of Insider Trading," *Journal of Business Ethics* 8 (November 1989). In "Justice and Insider Trading," *Journal of Applied Philosophy* 10, no. 2 (1993), Richard L. Lippke assesses insider trading from a broader moral and socioeconomic perspective. Two economists look at the issue in Yulong Ma and Huey-Lian Sun, "Where Should the Line Be Drawn on Insider Trading Ethics?" *Journal of Business Ethics* 17 (January 1998).

◆

CHAPTER ELEVEN

Business and Environmental Ethics

W. Michael Hoffman

W. Michael Hoffman, professor of philosophy at Bentley College, contends that business has an ethical responsibility to the environment that goes beyond merely obeying environmental laws, and that it must participate actively and creatively in solving our environmental problems. To be sure, profitability and protecting the environment can go hand and hand. However, there is a risk, Hoffman argues, in enticing business to the environmental cause solely on the basis of self-interest just as there is a risk in encouraging business to behave ethically solely on the grounds that good ethics is good business. Although he agrees that an enlightened understanding of human self-interest can justify policies that preserve and protect the environment, Hoffman nevertheless advocates a biocentric, rather than a human-centered, approach to environmental ethics.

THINGS TO CONSIDER

1. Norman Bowie asserts two points about business and the environment. What are they?
2. Hoffman writes that Bowie is responding to two extreme positions. Explain what they are.
3. What is Hoffman's response to the contention that the real burden for environmental change lies with consumers, not corporations?
4. Explain why Hoffman is against basing business ethics on the idea that "good ethics is good business."
5. What's the difference between the "biocentric" and the "homocentric" approaches to environmental ethics? What question is raised by the "last man" example?

From *Business Ethics Quarterly* 1 (April 1991). Copyright © 1991 The Society for Business Ethics. Reprinted by permission. Some notes omitted.

Albert Gore [has] said, "the fact that we face an ecological crisis without any precedent in historic times is no longer a matter of any dispute worthy of recognition." The question . . . is not whether there is a problem, but how we will address it. This will be the focal point for a public policy debate that requires the full participation of two of its major players—business and government. The debate must clarify such fundamental questions as: (1) what obligation does business have to help with our environmental crisis? (2) what is the proper relationship between business and government, especially when faced with a social problem of the magnitude of the environmental crisis? and (3) what rationale should be used for making and justifying decisions to protect the environment? Corporations, and society in general for that matter, have yet to answer these questions satisfactorily. In the first section of this paper I will briefly address the first two questions. In the final two sections I will say a few things about the third question.

I.

. . . Norman Bowie [has] offered some answers to the first two questions.

> Business does not have an obligation to protect the environment over and above what is required by law; however, it does have a moral obligation to avoid intervening in the political arena in order to defeat or weaken environmental legislation.[1]

I disagree with Bowie on both counts.

Bowie's first point is very Friedmanesque.[2] The social responsibility of business is to produce goods and services and to make profit for its shareholders, while playing within the rules of the market game. These rules, including those to protect the environment, are set by the government and the courts. To do more than is required by these rules is, according to this position, unfair to business. In order to perform its proper function, every business must respond to the market and operate in the same arena as its competitors. As Bowie puts this:

> An injunction to assist in solving societal problems [including depletion of natural resources and pollution] makes impossible demands

on a corporation because, at the practical level, it ignores the impact that such activities have on profit.[3]

If, as Bowie claims, consumers are not willing to respond to the cost and use of environmentally friendly products and actions, then it is not the responsibility of business to respond or correct such market failure.

Bowie's second point is a radical departure from this classical position in contending that business should not lobby against the government's process to set environmental regulations. To quote Bowie:

> Far too many corporations try to have their cake and eat it too. They argue that it is the job of government to correct for market failure and then they use their influence and money to defeat or water down regulations designed to conserve and protect the environment.[4]

Bowie only recommends this abstinence of corporate lobbying in the case of environmental regulations. He is particularly concerned that politicians, ever mindful of their reelection status, are already reluctant to pass environmental legislation which has huge immediate costs and in most cases very long-term benefits. This makes the obligations of business to refrain from opposing such legislation a justified special case.

I can understand why Bowie argues these points. He seems to be responding to two extreme approaches, both of which are inappropriate. Let me illustrate these extremes by the following two stories.

. . . Harvard Business School Professor George Cabot Lodge told of a friend who owned a paper company on the banks of a New England stream. On the first Earth Day in 1970, his friend was converted to the cause of environmental protection. He became determined to stop his company's pollution of the stream, and marched off to put his new-found religion into action. Later, Lodge learned his friend went broke, so he went to investigate. Radiating a kind of ethical purity, the friend told Lodge that he spent millions to stop the pollution and thus could no longer compete with other firms that did not follow his example. So the company went under, 500 people lost their jobs, and the stream remained polluted.

When Lodge asked why his friend hadn't sought help from the state or federal government for stricter standards for everyone, the man replied that was not the American way, that government should not interfere with business activity, and that private enterprise could do the job alone. In fact, he felt it was the social responsibility of business to solve environmental problems, so he was proud that he had set an example for others to follow.

The second story portrays another extreme. A few years ago "Sixty Minutes" interviewed a manager of a chemical company that was discharging effluent into a river in upstate New York. At the time, the dumping was legal, though a bill to prevent it was pending in Congress. The manager remarked that he hoped the bill would pass, and that he certainly would support it as a responsible citizen. However, he also said he approved of his company's efforts to defeat the bill and of the firm's policy of dumping wastes in the meantime. After all, isn't the proper role of business to make as much profit as possible within the bounds of law? Making the laws—setting the rules of the game—is the role of government, not business. While wearing his business hat the manager had a job to do, even if it meant doing something that he strongly opposed as a private citizen.

Both stories reveal incorrect answers to the questions posed earlier, the proof of which is found in the fact that neither the New England stream nor the New York river was made any cleaner. Bowie's points are intended to block these two extremes. But to avoid these extremes, as Bowie does, misses the real managerial and ethical failure of the stories. Although the paper company owner and the chemical company manager had radically different views of the ethical responsibilities of business, both saw business and government performing separate roles, and neither felt that business ought to cooperate with government to solve environmental problems.

If the business ethics movement has led us anywhere in the past fifteen years, it is to the position that business has an ethical responsibility to become a more active partner in dealing with social concerns. Business must creatively find ways to become a part of solutions, rather than being a part of problems. Corporations can and must develop a conscience, as Ken Goodpaster and others have argued—and this includes an environmental conscience.[5] Corporations should not isolate themselves from participation in solving our environmental problems, leaving it up to others to find the answers and to tell them what not to do.

Corporations have special knowledge, expertise, and resources which are invaluable in dealing with the environmental crisis. Society needs the ethical vision and cooperation of all its players to solve its most urgent problems, especially one that involves the very survival of the planet itself. Business must work with government to find appropriate solutions. It should lobby for good environmental legislation and lobby against bad legislation, rather than isolating itself from the legislative process as Bowie suggests. It should not be ethically quixotic and try to go it alone, as our paper company owner tried to do, nor should it be ethically inauthentic and fight against what it believes to be environmentally sound policy, as our chemical company manager tried to do. Instead business must develop and demonstrate moral leadership.

There are examples of corporations demonstrating such leadership, even when this has been a risk to their self-interest. In the area of environmental moral leadership one might cite DuPont's discontinuing its Freon products, a $750-million-a-year business, because of their possible negative effects on the ozone layer, and Procter and Gamble's manufacture of concentrated fabric softener and detergents that require less packaging. But some might argue, as Bowie does, that the real burden for environmental change lies with consumers, not with corporations. If we as consumers are willing to accept the harm done to the environment by favoring environmentally unfriendly products, corporations have no moral obligation to change so long as they obey environmental law. This is even more the case, so the argument goes, if corporations must take risks or sacrifice profits to do so. . . .

Activities that affect the environment should not be left up to what we, acting as consumers, are willing to tolerate or accept. To do this would be to use a market-based method of reasoning to decide on an issue which should be determined instead on the basis of our ethical responsibilities as a member of a social community.

Furthermore, consumers don't make the products, provide the services, or enact the legislation which can be either environmentally friendly or unfriendly. Grassroots boycotts and lobbying efforts are important, but we also need leadership and mutual cooperation from business and government in setting forth ethical environmental policy. Even Bowie admits that perhaps business has a responsibility to educate the public and promote environmentally responsible behavior. But I am suggesting that corporate moral leadership goes far beyond public educational campaigns. It requires moral vision, commitment, and courage, and involves risk and sacrifice. I think business is capable of such a challenge. Some are even engaging in such a challenge. Certainly the business ethics movement should do nothing short of encouraging such leadership. I feel morality demands such leadership.

II.

If business has an ethical responsibility to the environment that goes beyond obeying environmental law, what criterion should be used to guide and justify such action? Many corporations are making environmentally friendly decisions where they see there are profits to be made by doing so. They are wrapping themselves in green where they see a green bottom line as a consequence. This rationale is also being used as a strategy by environmentalists to encourage more businesses to become environmentally conscientious. . . . The highly respected Worldwatch Institute published an article by one of its senior researchers entitled "Doing Well by Doing Good" which gives numerous examples of corporations improving their pocketbooks by improving the environment. It concludes by saying that "fortunately, businesses that work to preserve the environment can also make a buck."[6]

In a recent Public Broadcast Corporation documentary entitled "Profit the Earth," several efforts are depicted of what is called the "new environmentalism," which induces corporations to do things for the environment by appealing to their self-interest. The Environmental Defense Fund is shown encouraging agribusiness in Southern California to irrigate more efficiently and profit by selling the water saved to the city of Los Angeles. This in turn will help save Mono Lake. EDF is also shown lobbying for emissions trading that would allow utility companies that are under their emission allotments to sell their "pollution rights" to those companies that are over their allotments. This is for the purpose of reducing acid rain. Thus, the frequent strategy of the new environmentalists is to get business to help solve environmental problems by finding profitable or virtually costless ways for them to participate. They feel that compromise, not confrontation, is the only way to save the earth. By using the tools of the free enterprise system, they are in search of win-win solutions, believing that such solutions are necessary to take us beyond what we have so far been able to achieve.

I am not opposed to these efforts; in most cases I think they should be encouraged. There is certainly nothing wrong with making money while protecting the environment, just as there is nothing wrong with feeling good about doing one's duty. But if business is adopting or being encouraged to adopt the view that good environmentalism is good business, then I think this poses a danger for the environmental ethics movement—a danger that has an analogy in the business ethics movement.

As we all know, the position that good ethics is good business is being used more and more by corporate executives to justify the building of ethics into their companies and by business ethics consultants to gain new clients. For example, the Business Roundtable's *Corporate Ethics* report states:

> The corporate community should continue to refine and renew efforts to improve performance and manage change effectively through programs in corporate ethics. . . . [C]orporate ethics is a strategic key to survival and profitability in this era of fierce competitiveness in a global economy.[7]

And, for instance, the book *The Power of Ethical Management* by Kenneth Blanchard and Norman Vincent Peale states in big red letters on the cover jacket that "Integrity Pays! You Don't Have to Cheat to Win." The blurb on the inside cover promises that the book "gives hard-hitting, practical, *ethical* strategies that build profits, productivity, and long-term success." Whoever would have guessed that business ethics could deliver all that! In such ways business ethics gets marketed as the newest cure for what ails corporate America.

Is the rationale that good ethics is good business a proper one for business ethics? I think not. One thing that the study of ethics has taught us over the past 2,500 years is that being ethical may on occasion require that we place the interests of others ahead of or at least on par with our own interests. And this implies that the ethical thing to do, the morally right thing to do, may not be in our own self-interest. What happens when the right thing is not the best thing for the business?

Although in most cases good ethics may be good business, it should not be advanced as the only or even the main reason for doing business ethically. When the crunch comes, when ethics conflicts with the firm's interests, any ethics program that has not already faced up to this possibility is doomed to fail because it will undercut the rationale of the program itself. We should promote business ethics, not because good ethics is good business, but because we are morally required to adopt the moral point of view in all our dealings—and business is no exception. In business, as in all other human endeavors, we must be prepared to pay the costs of ethical behavior.

There is a similar danger in the environmental movement with corporations choosing or being wooed to be environmentally friendly on the grounds that it will be in their self-interest. There is the risk of participating in the movement for the wrong reasons. But what does it matter if business cooperates for reasons other than the right reasons, as long as it cooperates? It matters if business believes or is led to believe that it only has a duty to be environmentally conscientious in those cases where such actions either require no sacrifice or actually make a profit. And I am afraid this is exactly what is happening. I suppose it wouldn't matter if the environmental cooperation of business was only needed in those cases where it was also in business' self-interest. But this is surely not the case, unless one begins to really reach and talk about that amorphous concept "long-term" self-interest. Moreover, long-term interests, I suspect, are not what corporations or the new environmentalists have in mind in using self-interest as a reason for environmental action.

I am not saying we should abandon attempts to entice corporations into being ethical, both environmentally and in other ways, by pointing out and providing opportunities where good ethics is good business. And there are many places where such attempts fit well in both the business and environmental ethics movements. But we must be careful not to cast this as the proper guideline for business' ethical responsibility. Because when it is discovered that many ethical actions are not necessarily good for business, at least in the short run, then the rationale based on self-interest will come up morally short, and both ethical movements will be seen as deceptive and shallow.

III.

What is the proper rationale for responsible business action toward the environment? A minimalist principle is to refrain from causing or prevent the causing of unwarranted harm, because failure to do so would violate certain moral rights not to be harmed. There is, of course, much debate over what harms are indeed unwarranted due to conflict of rights and questions about whether some harms are offset by certain benefits. Norm Bowie, for example, uses the harm principle, but contends that business does not violate it as long as it obeys environmental law. Robert Frederick, on the other hand, convincingly argues that the harm principle morally requires business to find ways to prevent certain harm it causes even if such harm violates no environmental law.[8]

However, Frederick's analysis of the harm principle is largely cast in terms of harm caused to human beings and the violation of rights of human beings. Even when he hints at the possible moral obligation to protect the environment when no one is caused unwarranted harm, he does so by suggesting that we look to what we, as human beings, value. This is very much in keeping with a humanistic position of environmental ethics which claims that only human beings have rights or moral standing because only human beings have intrinsic value. We may have duties with regard to nonhuman things (penguins, trees, islands, etc.) but only if such duties are derivative from duties we have toward human beings. Nonhuman things are valuable only if valued by human beings.

Such a position is in contrast to a naturalistic view of environmental ethics which holds that natural things other than human beings are intrinsically valuable and have, therefore, moral standing. Some naturalistic environmentalists only include other sentient animals in the framework of being deserving of moral consideration; others include all things that are alive or are an integral part of an ecosystem. This latter view is sometimes called a biocentric environmental ethic as opposed to the homocentric view, which sees all moral claims in terms of human beings and their interests. Some characterize these two views as deep versus shallow ecology.

The literature on these two positions is vast and the debate is ongoing. The conflict between them goes to the heart of environmental ethics and is crucial to our making of environmental policy and to our perception of moral duties to the environment, including business'. I strongly favor the biocentric view. And although this is not the place to try to adequately argue for it, let me unfurl its banner for just a moment.

A version of R. Routley's "last man" example[9] might go something like this: Suppose you were the last surviving human being and were soon to die from nuclear poisoning, as all other human and sentient animals have died before you. Suppose also that it is within your power to destroy all remaining life, or to make it simpler, the last tree which could continue to flourish and propagate if left alone. Furthermore, you will not suffer if you do not destroy it. Would you do anything wrong by cutting it down? The deeper ecological view would say yes because you would be destroying something that has value in and of itself, thus making the world a poorer place.

It might be argued that the only reason we may find the tree valuable is because human beings generally find trees of value either practically or aesthetically, rather than the atoms or molecules they might turn into if changed from their present form. The issue is whether the tree has value only in its relation to human beings or whether it has a value deserving of moral consideration inherent in itself in its present form. The biocentric position holds that when we find something wrong with destroying the tree, as we should, we do so because we are responding to an intrinsic value in the natural object, not to a value we give to it. This is a view that argues against a humanistic environmental ethic and urges us to channel our moral obligations accordingly.

Why should one believe that nonhuman living things or natural objects forming integral parts of ecosystems have intrinsic value? One can respond to this question by pointing out the serious weaknesses and problems of human chauvinism.[10] More complete responses lay out a framework of concepts and beliefs which provides a coherent picture of the biocentric view with human beings as a part of a more holistic value system. . . . In the final analysis, environmental biocentrism is adopted or not depending on whether it is seen to provide a deeper, richer, and more ethically compelling view of the nature of things.

If this deeper ecological position is correct, then it ought to be reflected in the environmental movement. Unfortunately, for the most part, I do not think this is being done, and there is a price to be paid for not doing so. Moreover, I fear that even those who are of the biocentric persuasion are using homocentric language and strategies to bring business and other major players into the movement because they do not think they will be successful otherwise. They are afraid, and undoubtedly for good reason, that the large part of society, including business, will not be moved by arguments regarding the intrinsic value and rights of natural things. It is difficult enough to get business to recognize and act on their responsibilities to human beings and things of human interest. . . .

A major concern in using the homocentric view to formulate policy and law is that nonhuman nature will not receive the moral consideration it deserves. It might be argued, however, that by appealing to the interests and rights of human beings, in most cases nature as a whole will be protected. That is, if we are concerned about a wilderness area, we can argue that its survival is important to future generations who will otherwise be deprived of contact with its unique wildlife. We can also argue that it is important to the aesthetic pleasure of certain individuals or that, if it is destroyed, other recreational areas will become overcrowded. . . .

In most cases, what is in the best interests of human beings may also be in the best interests of the rest of nature. After all, we are in our present environmental crisis in large part because we have not been ecologically intelligent about what is in our own interest—just as business has encountered much trouble because it has failed to see its interest in being ethically sensitive. But if the environmental movement relies only on arguments based on human interests, then it perpetuates the danger of making environmental policy and law on the basis of our strong inclination to fulfill our immediate self-interests, on the basis of our consumer viewpoints, on the basis of our willingness to pay. There will always be a tendency to allow our short-term interests to eclipse our long-term interests and the long-term interest of humanity itself. Without some grounding in a deeper environmental ethic with obligations to nonhuman natural things, then the temptation to view our own interests in disastrously short-term ways is that much more encouraged. The biocentric view helps to block this temptation.

Furthermore, there are many cases where what is in human interest is not in the interest of other natural things. Examples range from killing leopards for stylish coats to destroying a forest to build a golf course. I am not convinced that homocentric arguments, even those based on long-term human interests, have much force in protecting the interests of such natural things. Attempts to make these interests coincide might be made, but the point is that from a homocentric point of view the leopard and the forest have no morally relevant interests to consider. It is simply fortuitous if nonhuman natural interests coincide with human interests, and are thereby valued and protected. Let us take an example from the work of Christopher Stone. Suppose a stream has been polluted by a business. From a homocentric point of view, which serves as the basis for our legal system, we can only correct the problem through finding some harm done to human beings who use the stream. Reparation for such harm might involve cessation of the pollution and restoration of the stream, but it is also possible that the business might settle with the people by paying them for their damages and continue to pollute the stream. Homocentrism provides no way for the stream to be made whole again unless it is in the interests of human beings to do so. In short it is possible for human beings to sell out the stream.[11] . . .

Finally, perhaps the greatest danger that biocentric environmentalists run in using homocentric strategies to further the movement is the loss of the very insight that grounded their ethical concern in the first place. This is nicely put by Lawrence Tribe:

> What the environmentalist may not perceive is that, by couching his claim in terms of human self-interest—by articulating environmental goals wholly in terms of human needs and preferences—he may be helping to legitimate a system of discourse which so structures human thought and feeling as to erode, over the long run, the very sense of obligation which provided the initial impetus for his own protective efforts.[12]

Business ethicists run a similar risk in couching their claims in terms of business self-interest.

The environmental movement must find ways to incorporate and protect the intrinsic value of animal and plant life and even other natural objects that are integral parts of ecosystems. This must be done without constantly reducing such values to human interests. This will, of course, be difficult, because our conceptual ideology and ethical persuasion is so dominantly homocentric; however, if we are committed to a deeper biocentric ethic, then it is vital that we try to find appropriate ways to promote it. Environmental impact statements should make explicit reference to nonhuman natural values. Legal rights for nonhuman natural things, along the lines of Christopher Stone's proposal, should be sought. And naturalistic ethical guidelines, such as those suggested by Holmes Rolston, should be set forth for business to follow when its activities impact upon ecosystems.[13]

At the heart of the business ethics movement is its reaction to the mistaken belief that business only has responsibilities to a narrow set of its stakeholders, namely its stockholders. Crucial to the environmental ethics movement is its reaction to the mistaken belief that only human beings and human interests are deserving of our moral consideration. I suspect that the beginnings of both movements can be traced to these respective moral insights. Certainly the significance of both movements lies in their search for a broader and deeper moral perspective. If business and environmental ethicists begin to rely solely on promotional strategies of self-interest, such as good ethics is good business, and of human interest, such as homocentrism, then they face the danger of cutting off the very roots of their ethical efforts.

NOTES

1. Norman Bowie, "Morality, Money, and Motor Cars," *Business, Ethics, and the Environment: The Public Policy Debate,* edited by W. Michael Hoffman, Robert Frederick, and Edward S. Petry, Jr. (New York: Quorum Books, 1990), 89.
2. See Milton Friedman, "The Social Responsibility of Business Is to Increase Its Profits," *The New York Times Magazine* (September 13, 1970).
3. Bowie, 91.
4. Bowie, 94.
5. Kenneth E. Goodpaster, "Can a Corporation Have an Environmental Conscience," *The Corporation, Ethics, and the Environment,* edited by W. Michael Hoffman, Robert Frederick, and Edward S. Petry, Jr. (New York: Quorum Books, 1990).
6. Cynthia Pollock Shea, "Doing Well By Doing Good," *World-Watch* (November/December, 1989), 30.
7. *Corporate Ethics: A Prime Business Asset,* a report by The Business Roundtable, February, 1988, 4.
8. Robert Frederick, "Individual Rights and Environmental Protection," presented at the Annual Society for Business Ethics Conference in San Francisco, August 10 and 11, 1990.
9. Richard Routley and Val Routley, "Human Chauvinism and Environmental Ethics," *Environmental Philosophy,* Monograph Series, No. 2, edited by Don Mannison, Michael McRobbie, and Richard Routley (Australian National University, 1980), 121ff.
10. See Paul W. Taylor, "The Ethics of Respect for Nature," found in *People, Penguins, and Plastic Trees,* edited by Donald VanDeVeer and Christine Pierce (Belmont, CA: Wadsworth, 1986), 178–83. Also see R. and V. Routley, "Against the Inevitability of Human Chauvinism," found in *Ethics and the*

Problems of the 21st Century, edited by K. E. Goodpaster and K. M. Sayre (Notre Dame: University of Notre Dame Press, 1979), 36–59.

11. Christopher D. Stone, "Should Trees Have Standing?–Toward Legal Rights for Natural Objects," *Southern California Law Review* 45 (1972).
12. Lawrence H. Tribe, "Ways Not to Think About Plastic Trees: New Foundations for Environmental Law," found in *People, Penguins, and Plastic Trees,* 257.
13. Holmes Rolston, III, *Environmental Ethics* (Philadelphia: Temple University Press, 1988), 301–13.

REVIEW AND DISCUSSION QUESTIONS

1. What are the most serious environmental problems facing us today? What do you see as their causes?
2. Critically assess Bowie's position. What might be said in favor of it? What problems, if any, do you see with it?
3. Hoffman believes that "business has an ethical responsibility to become a more active partner in dealing with social concerns." Do you agree with the quoted statement? Explain why or why not. Does business have an obligation to help solve our environmental problems?
4. Is it true that good ethics is good business? If it is, then what, if anything, is wrong with basing business ethics on this fact?
5. Do you agree with Hoffman that it is risky to encourage business to "adopt the view that good environmentalism is good business"? In your view, is there a conflict between environmentalism and profitability?
6. Compare the homocentric and the biocentric approaches. What considerations might be advanced for and against each? Does nature as a whole or specific parts of the natural world (such as ancient redwoods or the Grand Canyon) have intrinsic value (that is, are they valuable for their own sake), or do they have value only because human beings value them? If what is in the best interests of human beings is usually what is in the best interest of the rest of nature, does it matter which position we adopt?
7. With regard to preserving and protecting the environment, who has the most important role to play—government, individual consumers, or business?

SUGGESTIONS FOR FURTHER READING

Two good surveys of business and environmental ethics are Joseph R. DesJardins, "Environmental Responsibility," in Norman E. Bowie, ed., *The Blackwell Guide to Business Ethics* (Blackwell 2002), and Thomas Heyd, "Environmental Ethics and the Workplace: A Call to Action," in Robert A. Larmer, ed., *Ethics in the Workplace: Selected Readings in Business Ethics,* 2nd ed. (Wadsworth 2002). For Norman Bowie's views, see his "Money, Morality, and Motor Cars," in W. Michael Hoffman, Robert Frederick, and Edward S. Petry, Jr., eds., *Business, Ethics, and the Environment: The Public Policy Debate* (Quorum 1990). See also Joel Reichart and Patricia H. Werhane, eds., *Environmental Challenges to Business* (Philosophy Documentation Center 2000), and Amory B. Lovins, L. Hunter Lovins, and Paul Hawken, "A Road Map for Natural Capitalism," *Harvard Business Review* 77 (May–June 1999).